Written, edited and designed by the editorial staff of ORTHO Books.

Special consultants:
Elvin McDonald
James K. McNair
William C. Mulligan

S0-DHV-512

House plants Indoors/Outdoors

Contents

2 Living with plants all around

6 The basics of container gardening

22 The best outdoor gardens begin indoors

30 How to rescue the last flowers of Summer

32 Little gardens anyone can grow

38 You don't have to be rich to have a greenhouse

42 Whatever happened to Winter?

46 King Louis will have nothing on you

48 Figs—one to eat, many to enjoy

50 Shrubs on the move

56 Flowers every day

62 Summer flowers, winter sleepers . . . and vice versa

66 Ferns, philodendrons, palms and other foliage plants

84 Try something new

90 Mini-encyclopedia of house plants

96 Department of resources

Index Inside back cover

1

Living with plants all around

Gardening in containers is a way of life. The mobility of container plants can make your very personal world better.

Many people stumble onto the rewarding pleasure of container gardening when they receive a gift plant all wrapped in foil and tied with a florist's bow. Suddenly you feel like the new parent of something alive. Don't panic! Just get rid of that foil and bow—then let's explore the fascinating world of house plants.

Plants have been cultivated in containers for centuries, but only in the last few years has the idea really caught on. Today it seems there are plant shops, florists and nurseries on every corner. Even the supermarkets and department stores have sections devoted to green, growing things. Even as we were preparing this copy, one of our editors came back from lunch carrying two large hanging basket plants she had bought from a man selling from a parked van right in front of our building.

Commercial growers report to us that they find it difficult to grow plants fast enough to meet the demand. Specimen trees are becoming scarce. Small plants are being turned out with almost assembly-line

◁

Top: A container garden in the Manhattan living room of garden editor Elvin McDonald. Lower left: Potted primroses lend color to a terrace garden. Lower right: Chrysanthemum in redwood tub is mobile for stage center attention indoors or outdoors as desire and climate dictate.

speed by growers. Our scouts found it difficult to locate some of the old favorite house plants.

The fact is, we need living plants all around us for they help to purify the atmosphere, they give us oxygen and they also absorb noise pollution.

A living plant also responds to the individual person who cares for it. This doesn't mean you have to whisper sweet nothings to it, or play rock or Bach music. It does mean that when you adopt a plant as your own, you become responsible for its well being. Plants growing directly in the ground are less dependent than those growing in containers, which is partly why so many people are growing plants in pots today. They want to feel closer to nature, and not everyone wants to or can afford to go all the way back to the farm. All you need is one seed and a pot of moist soil and you can experience all the good things of plant life, nature's perfect cycle and the heady aroma of healthy soil.

Trends in container gardening

In this book we have assembled the latest available information and ideas on house plants. A leader of our group is a well-known garden editor and writer. His work brings him in contact with what's happening throughout the world in all phases of container gardening. In these pages he shares his wealth of knowledge with you.

Another of our consultants recently moved to the West Coast from New York City where he headed a horticultural design studio catering to specialty stores, architects, interior designers and a few select well-known clients. He reported to us the trends of growing all kinds of living things in addition to the time-honored indestructibles:

"I have encouraged people to have a personal 'celebration of nature,' and to see plants in a new light relating to the whole ecology movement. My plantings emphasized the organic qualities—roots seen through simple clear-glass shapes, stratified layers of earth, stems pushing through the soil, buds, bulbs, sprouts—all the wonders of growth.

"Many of my clients planned their total living environment around their plants. One international banker collected only giant unusual specimens, calling them 'living sculptures.' Others filled their apartments with plants of all sizes, leaving only room for minimal, essential furnishings."

Growing all kinds of flowers, shrubs and trees in containers has always been practiced in estate gardens

everywhere, but shortly after World War II the practice became generally popular in California. Slowly but surely it has spread over the entire country. People who wouldn't dream of committing their leisure time to a perennial flower border, or even a big lawn, grow pots, tubs and baskets of plants in outdoor living areas.

Prim rows of windowsill pots have given way to indoor trees with branches reaching over sofas and chairs. Instead of draperies at the windows, today we see hanging baskets in many homes and apartments. And in interior spaces where bright light or sun never reaches, fluorescent and cool beam incandescent lights provide life-giving rays for real plants.

Our mobility as a people has also influenced container gardening. Magnificent container gardens all over Europe have inspired us to do the same. And as more of us grow plants in containers, the demand has grown for a greater selection. Wholesale growers in warm-weather climates now find it profitable to propagate more unusual plants, and daily these are trucked or air-freighted all over the country. The carissa or Natal plum flowering and fruiting in a container in Southern California on Friday may well be found in a retail nursery in New England the following week. Shortly thereafter it will be taken home to be planted in a handsome terra-cotta pot, or possibly turned into a bonsai. In this northern climate it will spend the summer outdoors, the winter indoors. This indoor-outdoor mobility of container plants is the theme of this book.

Early morning sun lights pebble tray garden. With a little discipline pets and plants can thrive in peaceful co-existence.

What is a house plant?

Mother Nature does not grow any "house plants" as such. All plants grown in containers indoors are native to an outdoor environment somewhere. Given favorable atmos-

An unusual combination—chrysanthemums and succulents—in a mobile garden featuring found stones, cement sculpture and weathered boards.

Interesting shapes in terracotta planters for a contemporary garden of flowers, vegetables and foliage plants. Check builder's supply houses for clay tile pipes, flues and joints in many unusual shapes. They make great containers and are less expensive than many imported planters. The gardener also adds basket plants on background fence.

pheric conditions, almost anything that grows can be a "house plant."

Our revolution in plant distribution makes it possible to enjoy growing plants native to other habitats in almost any climate. Grow exotic bulbs in and out of season. Plant herbs and vegetables, not only to enjoy the harvest, but for the beauty of their foliage and flowers, as well as their fragrance.

Citrus and other fruiting trees can provide people everywhere with a year-round orangerie. We grow arid desert species on window sills thousands of miles from the desert. Many outdoor shrubs and vines can be grown indoors, or, better yet, given mobility for indoor/outdoor cycles according to weather conditions. Many plants unheard of by our grandparents are available from specialty growers or importers through local outlets or mail order. (Check our source list on page 96.)

Houses are built to give their owners a more comfortable climate. More often than not, the indoor climate is characterized by low humidity and a fairly even 72° temperature—not exactly the ideal conditions for growing plants.

On the other hand, if you wanted to grow perfect house plants you could convert your living room into a

greenhouse—the plants would thrive and the people would suffer. In between these two extremes a climate can be created where people and plants can live comfortably under the same roof—all it takes is an understanding of an indoor climate and the requirements of a plant growing indoors. (See our section of house plant basics beginning on page 7.)

All houses have different atmospheres that will determine what you can grow and how to care for it. We are not telling you what to grow, but offering you a wide selection, along with basic gardening guidelines. Find what works for you with the resources available—indoors or outdoors—for growing in containers.

Whether you want to grow one tomato in a pot or a whole garden, we think you'll find the how-to information in this book, along with ideas for plants you can grow and ways to enjoy them. All of us who have worked on this book garden in containers. Some of us live in city apartments, others in private houses. We know the fun and the rewards of container gardening, and the problems too. In these pages we have attempted to impart our enthusiasm along with the varieties and cultural how-to it takes to live with mobile plants.

Judy Randlett's New York City apartment garden, first published in Madamoiselle, recently won top honors in the Burlington House Awards for American Gardeners. She uses hanging basket plants and container grown plants of all types throughout her open space. Judy says, "The greenery adds harmony and peace to my existence." She trades cuttings with friends and carries her plants with her in a truck when she goes on vacations, to be sure they are well cared for. Her feelings are shared by a large number of young gardeners throughout the country.

Upper left: A young California couple constructed planters from Chinese import crates for a terraced garden of flowers, vegetables and herbs which can be regrouped in infinite ways. Lower left: Forced bulbs brighten the usually drab mid-winter scene in most of the country. Lower middle: Year-round fruiting trees are grown in inexpensive prefab greenhouses. You can also grow them in good indoor light. Right: An orchid collector selects species to give bloom throughout the year.

Los Angeles horticultural designer James McNair adapted an industrial shelving unit of stainless steel for indoor/outdoor mobility. The rubber casters make moving easy. On the left the 'plantcart' goes to fresh air and light. Watering is simple with a hose. Moisture trickles through the open shelves which also circulate air like a tiered greenhouse. Indoors the esthetic quality of the unit is emphasized, changing locations as whim dictates. A cool-beam lamp lights plants at night.

The basics of container gardening

The "how to" of growing plants in containers. Explore the elements—light, soil, moisture, temperature and food. Also tips for good health and propagation.

The single most important basic to remember about container gardening is this: The roots of the plant are confined to the container. They cannot search deeper or wider for sustenance. The plant depends on you for food and water, the same as a pet dog. Fortunately, plants do not have to be walked. In the pages that follow, you will find explicit directions for growing plants in containers. There are sections on light, temperature, humidity, soil, water, feeding, handling dormancy, potting and repotting, pruning and grooming, plus a section on problems and how to solve them.

Selecting plant containers

Pots and other containers suitable for plants are all around us. You can spend a fortune for a piece of export china in which to show off your finest fern or flowering plant, but you can also spend nothing and have a fine container. For example, you can start seeds and cuttings in the bottom third of a milk carton, or in a plastic dish that held margarine. In between

◊
Lath house with large potting table is the perfect workspace for container gardening basics.

these extremes is every imaginable kind of container for use indoors or outdoors, resting on any surface or hanging.

Clay pots

These classic, time-honored containers are hard to beat. They range in sizes from 2 to 18 inches in diameter, or more, and traditionally they have been available with saucers to match. The present rage for gardening has created a critical shortage and saucers are scarce. One thing is for certain, don't throw away a good clay pot or saucer. Before you place a plant in clay, soak the pot in a pail or basin of water—preferably for several hours. Otherwise, the thirsty, dry clay will rob needed moisture from the soil and the roots of your plant. When clay pots are not in use and when you have a spare moment, use a stiff brush and warm water to scrub them clean. You can also run them through the dishwasher.

A WORD OF CAUTION. Moisture seeps through clay saucers. In time it will mar wood and rot carpeting. A round of half-inch cork cut to fit under the saucer will dissipate the moisture. Plastic and glazed ceramic saucers present no problems.

Glazed pottery

Many containers can be highly decorative, especially for indoor plants. There are exquisite cachepots, some with, some without, drainage holes. Most have a distinct Oriental feeling which adapts surprisingly well to almost any kind of décor. Many nurseries and garden centers now stock an array of pots and trays for bonsai, and these can also be used for other plants or for miniature landscapes. If you select a container that does not have a drainage hole, the best practice is to grow the plant in a slightly smaller clay or plastic pot with drainage holes, and simply slip this inside the more decorative container. To camouflage the edges of the utilitarian pot, carpet the surface with florists sheet moss, water-polished stones or small shells.

Plastic pots and baskets

These types of containers have the distinct advantage of being lightweight. They are generally less expensive than clay and come in the same range of sizes. On a limited budget you can achieve a great look simply by using all white plastic pots. The ones in bright colors tend to be garish unless a scheme is worked

out with care. Terra-cotta colored plastic is the most attractive, especially for hanging baskets.

Wooden boxes or planters

Made of rot-resistant redwood or cypress, wooden planters are great-looking and also long-lasting. Unfortunately, the commercial product is seldom well designed and all too often is held together by

Plant collection in classic clay pottery.

quick-to-rust metal banding. The better way is to build, or have built, your own wooden planter boxes, sized to fit your particular needs. Don't overlook marine plywood as a relatively inexpensive material for making planters. Plans for building your own containers are available from California Redwood and American Plywood. See page 96.

Baskets

There are many kinds that make great holders for plants, but all of them rot quickly when subjected to constant moisture. If the basket is purely for show, to hide a utilitarian pot, be sure to use a saucer inside to collect excess water. If you wish to plant flowers, herbs or vegetables directly in a sizeable fruit basket, line it first with heavy-duty polyethylene plastic. Since these are not very strong containers, it is best to fill them only with one of the lightweight soilless mediums.

Hanging baskets

These can be clay, plastic, pottery or wire. The utilitarian plastic baskets sold by the hundreds of thousands are excellent containers, but not very attractive. You can slip slightly larger woven baskets around them, however, for decorative effect. We found many beautiful hangers in retail shops. You might like to make one from macrame, metal or plastic with hobby shop materials.

Meeting light requirements

Photosynthesis, the process by which plants grow, is triggered by light. Plants vary in the amount they need, but most perform satisfactorily in a wide range of intensities. For indoor gardening, there are four basic light categories:

Sunny areas receive at least 5 hours of direct sunlight in winter. Usually a window facing southeast, south or southwest admits this amount of light.

Semisunny locations receive 2 to 5 hours of sun each day in winter. Windows facing east or west belong here.

Semishady places have bright, open light, but little or no direct sunlight.

Shady areas receive no sunlight, but have light strong enough to cast a shadow.

How much light you have

Many things affect how much light comes in your windows. Where you live is important. For example, in the Rocky Mountains, sunlight in winter is much more intense than in New England. Smoke from local industry may make sunny days hazy. Trees and shrubs will cut down on light—can make a south, east or west window suitable for shade-loving plants. A white house next door, or cement driveway will give reflected light. Clean windows also mean more light. And don't forget—screens reduce light by as much as 30 per cent.

Day-length affects plants

When days are longest, plants will do noticeably better in your house; east- and west-facing windows will qualify as being sunny, while south-facing locations will need to be curtained so they do not admit too much sun. Day-length also determines when certain plants bloom.

Poinsettias and Christmas cacti set flower buds in autumn when days begin to shorten. Calceolarias and tuberous begonias set buds when days are increasing in length.

What you can do with the light you have

Because light plays the major role in healthy plant growth indoors, here are some lists of different plants for different lighting situations.

Plants for a sunny location

Very few plants can thrive in full, direct sunlight all day. Plants listed below need at least 5 hours of direct sunlight in winter. In areas where there is much snow, remember that rays of sun bouncing from snow can add up to 30 per cent additional light. Also white painted buildings or expanses of unshaded land can increase available sunlight. Gardeners in southern and western sunshiny states may find windows with southern and eastern exposures too bright for plants other than some cacti and other succulents. In other areas, southern or eastern exposures provide the required light for these plants. All the plants listed here will thrive in average house temperature and a slightly moist (humidity 30%) atmosphere.

Bulbs

Agapanthus*	Hyacinth*
Amaryllis*	Ixia*
Anemone*	Montbretia*
Caladium	Oxalis*
Calla lily*	Ranunculus*
Daffodil*	Tulbaghia*
Freesia*	Tulip*
Haemanthus*	

Flowering plants

Begonia	King's crown
Bird-of-Paradise	Lilies
Chrysanthemum	Miniature rose
Geranium	Passion flower
Gerbera	Poinsettia
Gloriosa	Shrimp plant

Foliage plants

Agave*	Herbs
Aloe*	Iresine
Aporocactus*	Jerusalem cherry
Astrophytum*	Joseph's coat
Bamboo	Kalanchoe*
Beaucarnea	Lobiva*
Caphalocereus	Mammillaria*
Coleus*	Notocactus*
Crassula	Opuntia
Echeveria*	Pereskia*
Echinocactus	Polyscias
Echinocereus*	Rebutia*
Echinopsis*	Saxifraga
Eucalyptus	Sedum
Euphorbia*	Stapelia*
Fatshedera	Stone plants*
Gymnocalycium*	Wax plant*
Gynura	

Shrubs

Acalypha*	Ixora*
Allamanda*	Myrtle*
Azalea*	Nandina
Bougainvillea*	Oleander*
Citrus*	Pittosporum*
Coccoloba	Privet*
Croton	Pyracantha*
Flowering maple*	Rhododendron*
Gardenia*	Silk oak
Hibiscus*	Stephanotis*
Hydrangea*	Sweet olive*

*Also produces significant flowers.

Plants for a semi-sunny location

Plants suggested in this category need 2 to 5 hours of sunlight in winter. In warm weather, they will do well in bright light with little or no direct sun. Provide a warm (60- to 80-degree), slightly moist (humidity 30% or more) atmosphere. These plants can be grown in an area that receives full sun if they are protected by a curtain, or if a sun-loving plant rises up to give some shade. In summer they do well in bright light with little or no direct sun. Most exposures fit this category, except those facing north or south. Also this seems to be the preferred lighting for a large portion of jungle-oriented tropical plants. Many of the flowering plants listed in the Sunny category can bloom in this light with additional light reflected from white buildings or open spaces outside.

Bulbs

Caladium	Hyacinth*
Clivia*	Narcissus*
Daffodil*	Tulip*

Flowering plants

Achimenes	Flame violet
African violet	Gloxinia
Calceolaria	Impatiens
Christmas cactus	King's crown
Cineraria	Lipstick vine
Crossandra	Orchids
Cyclamen	Shrimp plant

Foliage plants

Asparagus	Liriope*
Beaucarnea	Norfolk Island Pine
Begonia*	Palms
Brassaia	Pandanus
Bromeliads*	Pellionia
Chlorophytum	Peperomia
Cissus	Philodendron
Coleus	Pilea
Columnea*	Pleomele
Crassula	Pothos
Cyperus	Prayer plant*
Dizygotheca	Rhipsalis
Dracaena	Rhoeo*
Euphorbia*	Saxifraga
Fatsia	Snake plant
Fatshedera	Spathiphyllum*
Ferns	String-of-pearls
Ficus	Swedish ivy
Fittonia	Syngonium
Gynura	Tolmiea
Haworthia	Tradescantia
Hypoestes	Wax plant*
Ivy, English	Zebra plant*
Joseph's coat	Zebrina

Shrubs

Ardisia*	Fuchsia*
Aucuba	Gardenia*
Camellia*	Nandina
Clerodendrum*	Pittosporum*
Coffea*	Podocarpus
Dipladenia*	Silk oak
Eleagnus*	Sweet olive*
Euonymus	Tibouchina*
Ficus	

*Also produces significant flowers.

Plants for a semi-shady location

Plants in this group thrive in bright, open light, but need little or no direct sunlight. They will succeed in a warm, slightly moist atmosphere. Most are grown primarily for foliage.

Bulbs	
Caladium	

Flowering plants	
Achimenes	Flowering tobacco
African violet	Impatiens
Christmas cactus	Orchids

Foliage plants	
Acorus	Ivy, English
Anthurium	Liriope*
Asparagus	Norfolk Island pine
Aspidistra	Palms
Begonia*	Pandanus
Brassaia	Pellionia
Bromeliads*	Peperomia
Chinese evergreen	Philodendron
Cissus	Pilea
Dracaena	Pothos
Dieffenbachia	Prayer plant*
Ferns	Selaginella
Ficus	Snake plant
Helxine	Spathiphyllum*
Hypoestes	Syngonium

Shrubs	
Ficus	Podocarpus
Pittosporum	

*Also produces significant flowers.

Plants for shaded locations

Many foliage plants will grow in an area that receives no sunlight. But there should be enough light to cast a shadow when you pass your hand across the area in which the plant will be placed. It's a good idea to rotate plants kept in poor light—give them a week or two of bright light, even 2 hours of morning sunlight, then let them have a sojourn in the dimly lighted place.

Foliage plants	
Asparagus	Ivy, English
Aspidistra	Liriope
Chlorophytum	Palms
Chinese evergreen	Philodendron
Cyperus	Pothos
Dieffenbachia	Selaginella
Dracaena	Snake plant
Ferns	Spathiphyllum*
Ficus	Syngonium

Shrubs	
Ficus	Podocarpus
Pittosporum	

*Also produces significant flowers.

Our hand-crafted light unit has an automatic timer to give 12 to 16 hours daily required light alternated with a rest period. Fluorescent light tubes can be installed in units such as this, mounted on ceilings or attached to shelves or bookcases.

Try gardening under artificial light

Fluorescent lights make it possible to have thriving plants in the places where you'll enjoy them most. Even your basement or attic can become a veritable greenhouse filled with beautiful flowers. Little money is needed to change a dimly lighted spot into an attractive display of healthy plants.

SUMMER ALL YEAR. Plants growing under fluorescent light don't have to cope with long periods of cloudy weather. Light intensity is the same in December as in June (provided tubes are replaced once every six to 12 months). Fluorescent light is cool. It never burns tender foliage.

KINDS OF FIXTURES. The basic set-up for growing plants under artificial light consists of a standard, industrial fluorescent unit with reflector that can be adjusted to stand 12 to 24 inches above the surface of a table or bench on which plants will be placed. For a sizable garden under lights, a prefabricated unit with several shelves makes a good investment. Using utilitarian steel shelving, you can also construct a similar and very inexpensive fluorescent-light garden.

HOW MUCH LIGHT? A fluorescent fixture with two or three 40-watt tubes in a reflector will light a growing area 2 by 4 feet. Two of these fixtures mounted parallel will illuminate a bench 3 by 4 feet. Two 8-foot, 2-tube industrial fluorescent fixtures suspended side by side will light a bench 3 by 8 feet. Fixtures with 20-watt tubes provide less light, but they are just as useful for growing plants, especially where space is limited and over a propagating box or terrarium.

CHOOSE THE RIGHT TUBE. There are many kinds of fluorescent tubes. While some growers swear by the special agricultural growth tubes, the time-proven combination of one Cool White with one Warm White is hard to beat. There are claims that flowering plants, especially sun-lovers respond to the addition of incandescent bulbs for the far-red light, but many successful growers have proved this is not necessary. Incandescents are highly inefficient and they also heat up and dry out the atmosphere.

PLANTS NEED SOME DARKNESS. Fluorescent tubes over plants are burned 12 to 16 hours out of every 24. Less time does not give good growth; more is of no benefit and may be harmful. Most growers turn lights on at 7 or 8 a.m., off at 10 or 11 p.m. An automatic timer should be used, both for your convenience and the well being of the plants.

PROVIDING HUMIDITY. The top of the table or bench under fluorescent lights should be framed so it can be covered to a depth of 1 to 2 inches with moist vermiculite, sand, pebbles or perlite. Surfaces may be waterproofed by lining with heavy-duty polyethylene, or by the use of a galvanized tray made to fit. There are also excellent plastic trays available which work well and look attractive.

PLANTS TO GROW. You can grow almost all indoor plants under fluorescent light, but be sure to check plant size. Dwarf geraniums, for example, are excellent under lights, but their full-size relatives take too much space.

INCANDESCENT LIGHT. Ordinary incandescent light is sometimes used as a supplement to fluorescents. However, this is not recommended. If you want to supplement daylight for a single large indoor plant or tree, or a collection, use cool beam incandescent floodlights which can be placed as close as 12 inches from the leaves, depending on wattage. Recommended are the General Electric Cool Beam and Sylvania's Cool-Lux. Use these only in ceramic sockets in bullet or track installations. For plants with little or no natural light, burn the spots 12 to 14 hours out of every 24. As a supplement to natural light, a few hours every evening should suffice.

The air surrounding your plants

Fresh, moist air helps plants thrive indoors. But it is unusual to find a home with prolonged temperatures below 70 degrees, or with relative humidity above 50 per cent.

Humidity. Excessive dryness in a home is harmful not only to plants, but can damage furniture and make the family uncomfortable. A cool vapor humidifier is an excellent way to increase humidity. Portable units can be placed where needed. Also you may want to have a humidifier installed as a part of your home's central heating system. We found one fairly inexpensive and well worth the cost for its effects on the plants, as well as on us.

Apart from these ways to increase humidity, it always helps to group plants, and to set the pots on trays of moist vermiculite, perlite or pebbles. Frequent misting helps humidity-loving plants to get moisture from the air as well as clean the leaves for better breathing. If spraying will harm floors, walls, or furniture, keep a large sheet of plastic handy to cover during spraying. I use a painter's drop cloth, available at hardware stores.

Temperature. Most plants will grow in a temperature range of 65 to 75°. A few degrees above or below

Inexpensive plastic hand sprayers build up humidity by frequent misting with water. Pressurized models are available.

these figures shouldn't be harmful. Plants from the tropics suffer when the temperatures go below 60°. On the other hand, plants such as cinerarias and camellias do best with a maximum temperature of 65°. For these cool-loving plants, you may be able to keep a sunny bedroom cool. Or, perhaps you have a sun porch that is cool—but does not freeze—in winter.

To increase humidity, group plants together on a large pot saucer or metal tray filled with pebbles. Keep water in tray just to top of pebbles. Don't allow pot bottoms to rest in water. A few chips of charcoal will keep water sweet.

Where winters are severe, tender plants close to windows may freeze. At night, put a piece of cardboard between the plants and the window, or move them to a warmer part of the room. Be sure to keep plants out of direct drafts of hot or cold air.

Air pollution. Fumes from manufactured gas cause plants such as African violets to drop their buds; geranium leaves to turn yellow and drop off. Natural gas is not harmful to plants, but many don't grow well in air that is frequently heavy with fumes from industrial and gasoline engines.

Good earth for containers

Unless you have a place to prepare potting soils, time to do the work, and a source of ingredients, it's a good idea to buy them ready-mixed.

Three or four basic soil mixtures will meet the needs of most plants.

A good all-purpose potting soil can be made by mixing together two parts garden soil, one part leaf mold and one part sand. This suits plants such as geraniums, amaryllis, dracaenas, palms and oxalis.

High humus content is important for such plants as African violets, begonias, philodendrons and azaleas. They do well in a mixture of equal

parts sand, peat moss, garden soil and leaf mold.

Plants from the desert need a gritty, lean-growing medium. Most cacti and other succulents will prosper in a mixture of one part garden soil, one part sand, one-half part decayed leaf mold and one-half part crushed clay flowerpot or brick. To each half bushel of this mixture, add a cup each of ground horticultural limestone and bone meal.

Air plants, called epiphytes, are cultivated in such mediums as osmunda fiber, unshredded sphagnum moss and chipped redwood bark. Most orchids and bromeliads are classed as epiphytes.

Take advantage of soil substitutes. Horticultural perlite is light as a feather and makes a perfect substitute for sand. Vermiculite, in place of leaf mold, will lighten and condition heavy, sticky soil and make it acceptable to plants that need a well-aerated soil. These inexpensive substitutes are already sterilized.

What growing "soilless" means

The newest trend in container gardening is to use soilless growing mediums. The most popular of these were perfected at Cornell University and the University of California. When these were first announced, the only way to take advantage of the information was to obtain the ingredients and do the mixing yourself. That is still possible, of course, and advisable if you need a large quantity. The mixes are available pre-mixed, however. The Cornell formula is available under such trade names as Jiffy Mix, Pro Mix and Redi-Earth. The University of California formula is available under the names First Step and Super Soil.

Both the Cornell and California mixes are similar. The main difference is that the Cornell uses vermiculite instead of the fine sand used in the California formula.

If you want to mix your own soilless growing medium, here is a recipe for Cornell mix:

> 4 quarts #2 grade vermiculite
> 4 quarts shredded peat moss
> 1 level tablespoon superphosphate
> 2 tablespoons limestone
> 4 tablespoons dried cow manure
> or steamed bone meal

It is most convenient to do your mixing in a large plastic pail. Be sure it is clean and dry before you add any of the ingredients. Also, it is a good idea to select a pail that has a tight-fitting lid. This will keep insects out and also allow you to keep the medium nicely moist, always ready for potting up.

The soilless mediums are not only sterile, and therefore conducive to healthy, disease- and pest-free root growth, but they are also lightweight.

This is especially important where large containers are involved, in rooftop gardening, and for hanging basket plantings.

Soil should be lightly moist for potting. If pre-mixed soil is dry, add water to the bag, close tightly and knead thoroughly to mix moisture through the planting medium as shown below.

Basic soilless mixes are available pre-packaged from your garden center under many trade names. Based on Cornell and University of California studies, these are formulated for all types of houseplants. Shown left to right: a high humus content mix for plants such as African violets, an all-purpose mix for most house plants, a formula suited to terrariums, and a gritty, lean-growing medium for cacti and other succulents. They are composed of various amounts of ingredients in text above.

How and when to water

Common sense is your most valuable guide in knowing when a potted plant needs to be watered. In respect to moisture at their roots, most like to have a growing medium that is nicely moist (not drippy or oozing with water; not dusty dry). When it is time to apply more moisture, the soil will have begun to dry out, and after watering it will be wet for a few hours. If you let a plant wilt before you apply moisture, you've waited too long. Dip sticks and moisture sensitive paper indicators

Time honored test of when to water is to insert finger about one inch below the soil surface. If dry, it indicates need for water.

Plants can be watered from below as in the photo above left. It is easier and faster to water from above. In either case, make sure it is thorough. After a few minutes pour off excess water which accumulates in the pot saucer. To retain moisture in a decorative pot, place the utilitarian pot inside and layer with florist's moss as shown.

are marketed to help you determine when it is time to water.

CONSTANT SATURATION is to the liking of a few plants. These include *Acorus,* bamboo, calla-lily, Chinese evergreen and *Cyperus.*

DESERT PLANTS (most cacti and other succulents) need a period of dryness between the times they receive moisture. However, drought loving plants grown in pots do need water more frequently than they would receive rain in their natural habitat; pots and other containers dry out more rapidly than the open ground.

To water or not to water

There are at least two ways to determine if a plant needs to have moisture applied to its roots:

By touch. *Insert finger about an inch into soil to feel if moist. Rub a bit of the surface layer of soil between your thumb and index finger. If dry powder results, watering is in order. If you get water- or mud-coated fingers, do not add water. If the soil you touch has a pleasing dampness, chances are good that watering won't be necessary for another 24 hours, maybe longer.*

By sight. *Wilted foliage usually signals a need for moisture. Conversely, it may mean that you have watered too much, and that the roots of the plant have contracted a rot.*

HOW OFTEN TO WATER. How frequently you find it necessary to water a plant varies with the season, size and kind of container and the plant species or variety itself.

SEASONS of the year when days are likely to be short, cloudy and moist, plants use less water than during sunny, long days of warmth. If temperatures can be kept favorable, and fertilizing continues, plants under fluorescent lights grow in autumn and winter as in spring.

SIZE AND KIND OF CONTAINER have much to do with how often a plant needs moisture. If the pot is small, moisture may be needed daily. Some plants need small pots. On the

other hand, if you can't keep a plant moist, probably it needs re-potting. Clay pots allow moisture to evaporate through the walls; glazed and plastic kinds transpire moisture only through the soil surface. Therefore, plants in them need water less often than those in clay.

Basic watering rules

Be thorough. Usually it is easier and faster to water container-grown plants from above. Submerging a pot in water to its rim, a procedure called bottom watering, takes more time, but it is good for plants you've allowed to dry out severely, and for those you get in full bloom from a florist. Submerging in a pail of water is the best way to water plants growing on slabs of tree-fern and also hanging baskets made of this material. Allow to drain, then return to growing space.

A severely dried out plant, such as this coleus, can be immersed in a pail of water to the pot rim. Wait until top soil is well moistened. Drain and return to its growing spot. After a short time it will return to its original healthy looking state.

Whether you apply moisture from above or below, pot saucers need to have excess moisture poured off within an hour after you apply water.

Water for indoor gardening

If you can drink the water where you live, then it is safe for pot plants. How you use the water is far more vital to plant life than the chemical content.

SOFTENED WATER MAY BE HARMFUL. Water softeners of the zeolite type can injure plants. This kind of softener replaces the calcium in water with sodium, which does not settle out, evaporate or become harmless. It will accumulate in houseplant soil to a harmful extent. If you have a water softener, install a tap in the

Following fertilizer manufacturer's directions could have prevented leaf burn from over feeding of this spider plant.

water line before it goes into the softener so you'll have unsoftened water for your plants.

WHERE WATER IS ALKALINE. In parts of the country where soil is very alkaline, and the water is hard, it is difficult to grow acid-loving plants. Generous use of acid peat moss and fertilizers which have an acid reaction will help offset the alkaline soil and water. Plants such as azaleas, gardenias and camellias will benefit from regular applications of an iron chelate (Sequestrene, for example) to keep the foliage a healthy dark green. When new foliage of these plants is yellow, water with a solution of one ounce iron sulfate in two gallons of water. Repeat at biweekly intervals until growth has normal color.

WATER TEMPERATURE IS IMPORTANT. Take the chill off water before you use it on house plants. Tropical plants are the most sensitive, but all may be harmed by having icy water applied either at the roots or or the foliage. Water for house plants should be barely warm or tepid—within 10° of the room temperature.

How and when to fertilize

Nitrogen, phosphates and potash are the three basic elements needed by plants. When you pick up a container of house plant fertilizer at your garden store, you see a combination of figures like 12-6-6. These numbers list in order the percentages of nitrogen, phosphates and potash in that fertilizer. In the one above there is 12 percent nitrogen, 6 percent phosphates and 6 percent potash.

BASICS ABOUT FERTILIZING. Container plants need regular feeding when they are in active growth. Most houseplant fertilizers on the market have been formulated for use every two weeks. This is more effective than large monthly doses. Follow container directions for rate and frequency.

Fertilizers are available in all types: water soluble pellets, powders and liquids; dry tablets and sticks to insert in the soil; time-release pellets. What ever kind you choose, read the label first and follow the directions. Make sure to always moisten the soil before adding any fertilizer to prevent root burn.

We talked to people involved in all phases of container gardening— nurserymen, plantsmen, retailers and hobbyists. All had their own favorite type of fertilizer. Some prefer dry formulas; one used only liquid fish emulsion; others used liquids for some plants, and prefer dry types for other plants.

Plants growing in synthetic soils need third- to half-strength fertilizer added every time they are watered.

TOO MUCH FERTILIZER causes leaf edges to turn brown in otherwise good growing conditions. Note the condition of the spider plant on the left. Excess plant food may cause lower leaves to drop prematurely, or the entire plant may wilt. If this happens to one of your plants, leach out the fertilizer by applying copious amounts of water, allowing the soil to drain, then pouring on more water. Or, you can wash the old soil from the plant roots and repot into fresh new soil.

FOLIAR FEEDING. This has been termed nature's way because in the tropics, certain jungle plants depend on nitrogen from rain, and bird droppings washed down on them from overhanging trees for nourishment. Read the labels at your garden store, and you will find kinds recommended

for foliar application. Apply every two to four weeks following container directions. Use as a supplement to liquid fertilizer applied directly to the soil.

Rest and recuperation

To some extent, nature's cycle for plant growth applies to those growing indoors the same as it does those outside. Shorter days and cooler temperatures induce dormancy. Excepting day length, centrally heated indoor environments offer a potentially endless summer. In fact, this is possible in a fluorescent-lighted garden where day length can be constant all year. However, even light-garden plants tend to have resting periods when growth slows, and when, consequently, they need less food and water.

TUBEROUS AND BULBOUS plants generally die to the ground while they rest. In cultivation we simply withhold food and water. However, not all bulbous plants die down. Potted agapanthus and tulbaghia, for example, stay leafy and green all year, sending up flowers after a time of active growth.

TROPICAL FOLIAGE PLANTS are more conscious of warm, moist air than seasonal periods of long and short days. Unless your home is unusually warm and humid in winter, plants like these will show a slowing of growth. Also, in these energy-conscious days when many thermostats are being lowered a few degrees, most tropicals will show a slow-down.

How to treat dormant plants

Most important to the health of your pot plants is that you realize when one is resting—or needs a rest. This is most likely to occur after a flush of new growth, or following a period of heavy flowering. Symptoms include absence of new growth, a "tired" appearance and yellowing, falling leaves.

When these symptoms occur, apply less water than usual. Keep the soil just moist, never really wet. Do not apply any fertilizer. In the winter, this is especially true of tropical plants situated where temperatures stay generally below 70 degrees. Cold, wet soil and feeding as in balmy weather kill countless pot plants. When a plant seems to be resting, do not repot. Wait, if you think this is necessary, until the plant starts some new leaf buds.

How and when to pot

A pot or other container holds the private underworld of a plant. What goes on down there in the darkness may be a mystery, but it is vital to what you see above the soil. Pot size comes first. The best potting soil in the world will have to work at a disadvantage if it is in a pot too small or too large for the plant.

The photos on these pages show steps in potting and repotting of most types of plants.

A general rule about pot size is to use a pot whose diameter at the top equals one-third to one half the height of the plant. This is illustrated

Gently tap pot on table edge to remove the plant and examine growing area. When roots fill the pot like this, it is an obvious sign to move the plant up to a size larger pot.

in the repotting of the marigold on this page.

In most instances it is advisable to move a plant up to a pot only one size larger than the previous one.

Clean pots help make gardening a special pleasure. They are also an inducement to neat, orderly storage according to size. Before you re-use any kind of pot that has been used before, scrub it clean. Plastic and glazed ones present no difficulty; treat them like dishes. To clean old, dirty clay pots, put them in a bucket and pour boiling water over them. Add a half cup of household bleach to the water and let stand for a few hours. After this soaking, it will be easy to scrub the pots so that they look like new. If you have an over supply of any standard type clay or plastic pot, give them to someone you know who gardens—either for fun or as a business.

When a plant is too large or difficult to transplant, like this mature cactus, you can remove as much soil as possible from the pot with the help of a hand spade. Then top-dress by refilling around the plant with fresh potting medium. Pack well to eliminate any air pockets around the plant roots. Water thoroughly.

In the series of photographs above we repot a straggly marigold. To determine size of the new pot, we choose a pot with a diameter one third the plant's height. Place some drainage material and soil in the pot as illustrated on the opposite page, add the plant and fill in with more soil. Pack firmly with fingers. Soak in a pail of water until thoroughly moistened. Trim off old leaves and spent blooms and enjoy a healthier looking and happier plant.

Below we wrap a prickly cactus with thick rolled newspaper for easier handling. Remember: those spines can stick through garden gloves. Use a spoon to add soil in tight places and a fork for packing soil. Clean soil from the plant surface with a small paintbrush. Don't water cactus for a few days.

Above: To repot a plant in a container without drainage, first remove the plant from its original container. Select the new one based on root size and the scale of the plant to container. Place a layer of broken pottery, small gravel or chips of charcoal in the bottom of the container. Add some sterile soil to the new pot. Loosen soil around roots of the plant. Place plant in position and add more soil to fill pot. Pack firmly with fingers to eliminate any air pockets which can cause root damage. Remember not to fill the pot so full of soil that there is no room left for watering. Succulents should not be watered for a few days after transplanting. Clean the plant and pot and add a ground mulch such as sand or gravel if desired.

Below: A top-heavy peperomia obviously in need of a new pot. Gently tap from its container. Place a piece of broken pottery over drainage hole in new container. This keeps soil from washing through hole and clogging drainage. Add some sterile potting medium, then the plant and fill in with more soil. Firm with fingers to eliminate air pockets. Water well to thoroughly moisten soil. Don't forget to soak clay pots prior to potting so they will not rob moisture from the newly planted roots. Here we add stakes for support of the tender stems. Use twist-em, yarn or soft cloth strips. Wrap the tie gently around the stem, then tie to the stake.

Good grooming techniques

Plants growing in pots and other containers have need for regular pruning and trimming back in order to keep them attractively shaped and to a size that makes them nice to have around. There are two methods for shaping most plants. One is called pinching, the other pruning.

Pinching

A simple operation you do with your thumb and forefinger to remove the young tip growth of a stem you want to branch out. For example, consider a young coleus plant. You have started it from seed or a cutting. If you let the plant grow without pinching, it would likely stay as one stem going straight up, eventually becoming lanky and weak. So, as soon as possible, nip out the growing tip. This causes dormant buds in the lower leaf axils to spring into active growth. Where you had one leader, now there will be two. After two or three weeks, you pinch the tips out of these two, and thus have a bushy plant of four; then eight, and finally 16 or more. Pinching is a handy thing to know about gardening. It works especially well for soft-stemmed plants like wax and angel-wing begonias, young geraniums and coleus.

Pruning

This is the means by which you can keep more-or-less woody plants to size and shape. You need a pair of small hand pruners to do this work. Plants like Chinese hibiscus, bougainvillea, gardenia and jasmine need pruning to keep the branch framework well-balanced and sturdy. After a flowering period, clip off long, weak branches that extend beyond the plant's overall shape.

Extras for a perfect container garden

Stakes, trellises and other means of support will help you have a collection of beautiful plants.

STAKING is a kind of art practiced by most commercial greenhouse men. Early in the life of a plant such as chrysanthemum, tuberous begonia or poinsettia, they tie each stem to a dark green bamboo or wooden stake. This technique was used for the tall, leggy peperomia on the preceding page. You can do this same sort of training in your container garden. Basics include staking early (you can keep a straight stem straight, but you may not be able to uncrook a crooked one), and using pieces of soft yarn, strips of cloth, or better still, the commercially prepared Twist-ems to hold stems to stakes.

TOTEM POLES are used as a means of support for some plants. These have various shapes including that of a cylinder, cone and ball. They are available as cut pieces of osmunda fiber, or you can make your own. Totems are ideal accessories for philodendrons, episcias and for training English ivy to grow into unusual shapes.

TRELLISES certainly have a place in container gardening, although they are not seen frequently. In the true sense of a trellis, you can put up a small wooden, wire or string one wherever you want a vine to decorate. In a sunny window, 'Heavenly Blue' morning-glories would make a cheerful drapery of green and bright blue. Black-eyed susan *(Thunbergia alata)* is another vine that will climb in a sunny window.

TOPSOIL should be kept raked and clean or cover with a layer of florist's sheet moss. Or use bark mulching, polished stones or gravel to add finishing touches.

Remove young tip growth from stems you want to branch out. Simply pinch out with your thumb and forefinger. This keeps the plant bushy and compact.

Brown or yellow edges can keep a plant from looking its best. Some browning is normal with many tropicals grown indoors. For esthetic reasons cut away the dried portion with sharp shears, following the original shape of the leaves. The cleaned-up foliage makes the plant look more attractive and does not harm its health or growth.

House plant pests and problems

Plant or Insect Looks Like This . . .		Problem Is . . .	What To Do . . .
Clusters of tiny bugs on new growth. Foliage is malformed and discolored.		Aphids.	Eradicate with pesticide such as ISOTOX Insect Spray or Malathion used as directed.
Leaf edges crisp and brown; quick withering of new growth.		Too much heat. Lack of humidity. Uneven soil moisture.	Lower temperature. Increase humidity. Avoid severely dry soil, then flooding.
Yellow lower leaves, some dropping off.		Improper growing conditions or age.	Avoid extremes in temperatures. Increase humidity. Give fresh air. Keep soil evenly moist. May need biweekly feeding. Be sure there are no gas leaks. After the precautions are taken, yellow leaf probably means it has matured and should be removed.
Nearly transparent spots on leaves caused by sucking of plant juices. Fine webs on underside of leaves. Look for tiny insects with magnifying glass.		Mites (Use magnifying glass or look for webs.)	Spray firm-leaved plants with forceful stream of water. Use aerosol spray which indicates use against red spider-mites.
Soft, slimy slugs on leaves or shell-covered snails around plants. Silvery streaks on foliage.		Slugs and snails.	Constant vigilance in plant sanitation. Use commercial slug bait.
Leaves appear lifeless; frequent wilting; requires daily watering.		Temperature too high; pot too small.	Put in cooler location. Change to larger container. Provide more sunlight or fluorescent light.
No flowers produced on plants which should bloom.		Lack of moisture or sunlight. Too much fertilizer.	Increase humidity. Keep evenly moist. Feed less; don't use high nitrogen fertilizer during blooming season.
Flower buds drop off before opening.		Improper growing conditions.	Avoid high or fluctuating temperatures. Be sure plant is out of drafts. Provide more humidity; mist twice daily.
Soft powder-covered insects look like specks of cotton on a plant.		Mealybugs.	If only a few, touch with cotton swabs dipped in alcohol. Sprays containing Malathion eliminate large colonies.
Soft or hard scales, brown or black, round, slow-moving insects.		Scale.	Small infestations on glossy-leaved plants can be removed by washing with strong soapsuds, or spray with aerosol pesticide recommended for eliminating these slow-moving insects.
Yellowish brown, sometimes silvery, spots on leaves.		Too much sun.	Give more shade.
White or yellowish rings and spots on foliage.		Cold water on leaves and roots.	Always use room temperature water. Don't let hot sun shine on foliage which has drops of water on it.

Planting hanging baskets

These are the trapeze artists of the plant world—they are at their best swinging, dangling or climbing. You can use pottery, wooden, wire or plastic hanging baskets (sold at local garden centers and by mail); or, suspend a small ceramic strawberry jar. Regular clay and plastic flowerpots may be used also; string, wire or chain used to hang them can serve also to hold a saucer in place so that pot will not drip water on floor. All kinds of decorative hangers can be used to give the planter a style of its own.

Line wooden baskets with aluminum foil so that soil won't wash through cracks. Wire and plastic baskets need to be lined first with coarse,

Variety in hanging plants is infinite. Here is a colorful trailing nasturtium.

unmilled sphagnum moss, or sheet moss, then filled with soil. Some growers go one step more, and give the moss liner a lining of burlap or a saucer to prevent soil erosion, then add soil and plants.

CULTURE OF HANGING BASKET PLANTS varies according to the plant. In general they need evenly moist soil, good light, and average warmth (60 to 80°). Water by immersing container at sink, or in pail. (Shown bottom right). Allow to soak, then drain sufficiently long that basket will not drip when it is re-hung.

Good hanging basket plants, of easy culture under average home conditions, include these:

Achimenes	Mahernia verticillata
Basket begonias	Pellionia
Ceropegia woodii	Philodendron
(rosary vine)	micans
Chlorophytum	Pilea depressa
(spider plant)	Plectranthus
Cissus	australis
Episcias	Scindapsus aureus
Ficus pumila	Sedum
or F. radicans	morganianum
Helxine	S. dasyphyllum
(baby's tears)	Senecio rowleyanus
Hoya carnosa	Wandering jew
Kalanchoe manginii	

To construct a hanging basket of wire, stuff the frame with moist sphagnum moss. You can add an extra lining of burlap at this point, if desired. Place a saucer (aluminum pie tin is perfect) in the bottom to keep soil from eroding. Pot the plant like any other container plant as shown on pages 14 and 15. Attach hangers and immerse in a large pail of water to thoroughly moisten. Half round wire frames are available for attaching to flat backgrounds. When planting wooden baskets line with foil or plastic to keep soil from washing through.

Propagating container plants

Plant multiplication or propagation which you do at home is one way to have lots of container plants—as unusual as you like—for very little money. And few aspects of gardening, or of any hobby for that matter, are as rewarding.

Starting from seed

Almost all seed catalogs offer seeds of house plants. You will find semperflorens begonias, geranium hybrids, gloxinias, cyclamen, kalanchoe and calla-lily. In more comprehensive listings you will find ferns, schefflera (brassaia), fuchsia, and jatropha. One to search out is silk-oak or grevillea which grows easily from seeds, first forming a fernlike bush, but rather quickly growing into a small tree just right for a bright spot indoors or as a patio specimen. Actually, the list of seeds available is practically endless. The most unusual seeds are often available through membership in one of the houseplant societies, for example the American Begonia Society or the American Gloxinia and Gesneriad Society; for addresses, see page 96. Certainly not to be overlooked are pits and seeds from the kitchen. You can grow fine foliage plants from avocado pits, citrus seeds or sprouted sweet and Irish potatoes and onions. Health food stores offer all kinds of seeds you can have fun sprouting. A handful of bean or pea seeds planted thickly on the surface of moist soil, either in a pot or shallow tray, will quickly give a lush patch of greenery. Actually, any seed is fair game for sprouting indoors, and you just may find a unique container plant. If in doubt as to how deep to plant, remember this general rule: Cover each seed to the depth of its own thickness. See pages 23-26.

How to root cuttings

Great grandmother called them "slips," we call them cuttings. To make one, all you do is break or cut off a healthy piece of growth, usually 4 to 6 inches long, but this varies according to the kind of plant. Strip or cut from the stem all leaves from the lower half of the cutting. Then, using your index finger or a pencil, make a hole in the rooting medium, insert the bare stem portion of the cutting, and firm it in place. Water well, encase the entire cutting and container in a plastic bag and set it in a shady, warm place. You can tell when roots have begun to grow because the foliage will perk up and the new plant will show signs of growing. Then you can remove the plastic cover, at first for an hour or two daily, then leave it off for several hours, and finally discard the cover and move the plant to a good growing area—sun if it is a sun-lover, shade if it is a shade plant. Transplant when the original pot is filled with roots.

Most house plants can be rooted in water and transplanted easily into soilless mixes. Here Steven McDonald is starting a Dracaena marginata cutting in a see-through pot which will allow him to watch root development. Lower leaves were removed from the stem before placing in water.

HOW TO AIR LAYER. This method is useful to salvage leggy plants which have become straggly looking and cannot grow lower leaves. First, cut into the stem and insert a wedge (such as prong of plastic fork) to pry stem open. Wrap in a plastic bag filled with damp sphagnum. Watch for roots to appear. Then cut stem off just below the new roots. Pot the rooted plant into its own container and enjoy a compact plant.

Different gardeners use different rooting mediums for cuttings. The easiest, most convenient is water, just a drinking glass of tap water. This old-fashioned method fell out of favor a few years ago, but seems to be making a comeback. Water-rooted cuttings transplant easily into one of today's soilless mixes such as the University of California or Cornell formula which are also available pre-mixed under such names as Jiffy Mix, Pro-Mix and Redi-Earth. When you pot up a cutting rooted in water, just be sure it is moistened well, and then cover it with plastic for a few days.

Cuttings also root well when planted directly in a soilless mix. Or you can use straight vermiculite, perlite, milled sphagnum moss, or a mix of these with peat moss. If you want to root a number of different cuttings, a clear plastic bread or shoe storage box makes an excellent propagator. Heat an ice pick to punch a few ventilation holes in the top. Add 2 inches of rooting medium in the bottom, moisten, then insert your cuttings. Put the lid on and set the box in bright light, but not direct sun, in a warm place. You can make a similar propagating box using a seed flat or fruit lug to hold the cuttings and a sheet of polyethylene plastic held up by wire coat hangers for the "greenhouse" cover.

If you read your seed catalogs closely, or wander down garden center aisles reading labels you may have noticed small containers of rooting hormones. These are excellent products. They do promote faster rooting and better root systems. You don't really need a rooting hormone for things like coleus and Swedish-ivy which root easily almost overnight, but for other plants, especially anything bordering on being woody—fuchsia and heliotrope, for example—they are recommended.

Some plants have the amazing ability to propagate themselves from a single leaf cutting. Best known for this is the African violet, but the same technique works for rex and some other rhizomatous begonias, gloxinias, sedums, kalanchoes, even some philodendrons (trailers or climbers) and peperomias.

poinsettia for example, allow them to dry or callous for a few hours. Simply place them on the kitchen cabinet or elsewhere out of direct sun. When the cut surface—base of the cutting—is dry, proceed with planting.

Tropical foliage plants that form a thick, trunklike stem, can be propagated from 4-inch cuttings. Remove any leaves and simply lay the "logs" on the surface of moist rooting medium in a propagating box. Roots and new leaf growth will sprout from

When leaves accidentally break from a plant, don't throw them out; start a new plant. African violets are among the plants that can be propagated from cuttings of a single leaf. Use a broken leaf or a leaf from the mother plant, make a sharp diagonal cut and place in moistened growing medium. Use the plastic cover to keep up humidity for a few days.

Take a cutting from a geranium plant with a sharp knife. Remove lower leaves and any excessive top growth. Use a pencil to make a hole in moistened soilless medium. Then place trimmed cutting in the pot. Cover for a few days with a plastic cup.

dormant eyes or leaf buds along the stem. This method works for Chinese evergreen (aglaonema), alocasia, dieffenbachia, dracaena, certain philodendrons and pleomele. These same plants can also be propagated by air-layering; see how-to photos, previous page.

Grafting of one species to another is a specialized technique. See cactus books.

Multiplying by division

When multiple stems emerge from the base of a plant, you can divide it. The wax begonia makes a good example as well as most bromeliads, cluster-forming succulents like certain sedums and crassulas and African violets that have not had suckers removed. Sansevierias also multiply this way; one healthy division sometimes fills the pot with others in a year's time. The easiest way to propagate by division is to take a sharp knife and slice down through the soil, severing a new plant from the old. Hopefully you will be able to get some roots along with it, but the main thing to remember is that you must get some of the main stem system, otherwise the new plant cannot live.

The other way to divide is to knock the entire plant out of its pot, and then, with your hands gently pull away the soil to fully expose the root system and framework of the plant. Cut or break apart the divisions and replant each one.

Division is also an excellent way to multiply your supply of amaryllis, some haemanthus, zephyranthes, fisherman's net *(Bowiea volubilis)*, tulbaghia and clivia. The sea- or pregnant-onion *(Urginea maritima)* forms pealike bulbils on the surface of the old bulb; all you have to do is pick these and plant them.

TUBER DIVISION is closely related to dividing plants with multiple basal stems or leaf rosettes. This works for large bulbs of gloxinia, gloxinera, tuberous begonia and caladium. Simply cut apart the tuber like a seed potato, being sure that every part

has a bud or "eye." Dust the cut surface with a fungicide then plant in moist rooting medium.

Rooting tree and shrub cuttings

Trees and shrubs can be propagated from softwood or hardwood cuttings. Softwood describes this year's growth taken early or midseason. Hardwood describes growth at the end of the season.

Softwood cuttings to try include abutilon, acacia, aralia, Norfolk Island pine, ardisia, blueberry, gardenia and rose. Ligustrum, pyracantha, forsythia, weigela and sweet-olive can also be rooted this way. Hardwood cuttings include azalea, rhododendron, boxwood, conifers or needle evergreens, grapes, dogwood and flowering trees.

SOFTWOOD CUTTINGS are prepared for planting the same as a house plant such as geranium or angel-wing begonia. They'll do best in a cool, moist, airy, bright atmosphere, but no direct sun until roots have formed. Some growers rig up a mist system with jets timed to mist the cuttings every few minutes.

HARDWOOD CUTTINGS are usually made in autumn, sometimes after frost has defoliated deciduous types. Dip the base of each cutting in rooting hormone, then plant. Cover with plastic or glass and keep in moderate coolness (60-70°). A cool fluorescent-lighted garden, perhaps in a basement, makes an ideal spot to root hardwood cuttings. Cold-hardy types such as evergreens can be planted in a cold frame.

SEED can be sprouted to start trees and shrubs. Kinds winter hardy in the North usually require a period of freezing temperatures, followed by warmth in order to break their dormancy. If you don't have a coldframe in which to do your planting, you can simulate winter and the stratification process in your freezer. Mix the seeds with moist sand and peat moss in a jar or plastic

container. Chill for two to four months, then plant in a warm, bright place.

There are seeds available of fine azalea hybrids—Kaempferi, Exbury, Mollis and Kurume, for example. These are tiny seeds that require the same treatment you would give gloxinias or begonias. In a range of 60 to 70° they will sprout in about three weeks.

Stolon propagation

Several common house plants grow stolons or runners, strawberry-fashion. These include *Saxifraga stolonifera* (strawberry-begonia), flame violets or episcias, some species of African violet, spider plant or *Chlorophytum* and the walking iris or *Neomarica*. One way to root these is to fill a small pot with moist rooting medium, draw it up alongside the mother plant and hairpin or tape the base of the stolon into place. Active new growth will signal that the baby has its own root system, and then you can sever it from the mother. The other way with stolons is simply to clip them off and insert the base of each in moist propagating medium, either in a community box or in an individual pot. Cover with glass or plastic film until new roots have formed.

Piggyback plant or tolmiea forms new plantlets on top of old leaves, and these can be rooted the same as stolons or runners.

Plantlets formed on stolons of the spider plant, above, and the piggyback plant, below, can be pinned into moist soil in a pot. Leave alongside mother plant until rooted, or separate and pin in its own pot.

The best outdoor gardens begin indoors

Get a head start on Spring by beginning early indoors—flowers, vegetables, herbs and foliage plants.

You can be more successful with many varieties of flowers and vegetables and at the same time extend the growing season in your garden by starting seeds indoors while there is still danger of frost, then transplanting them to the outdoor garden or containers. This plan works well for areas of the country with short growing seasons, but it is advantageous to warmer climates also because you can bring your garden into full bloom and productivity weeks ahead of time.

Vegetables such as broccoli, Brussels sprouts, cabbage, cauliflower, eggplant, peppers and tomatoes are recommended for the transplanting method. It gives them more time to complete their growth and produce

◁

A colorful carpet of potted primroses for an "instant" early spring garden.

earlier fruit of a higher quality. Also by starting plants from seeds indoors it is possible to have transplants of unusual vegetables and flowers that are not available at local plant markets. Even for the common varieties it is a money-saving method. Seeds cost only pennies in comparison with purchased plant seedlings.

By beginning the seed indoors some of the hazards common to seedlings—birds, insects, weeds and heavy rains—can be eliminated.

Starting the seeds

A seed is merely a container for a dormant tiny plant waiting for the right conditions to continue the life cycle. To achieve this it must be given a disease-free growing medium, proper warmth and moisture and adequate light for germination.

Don't start seeds too early. Consult our chart on page 26 for time it takes to germinate and grow plant to proper transplanting stage. Count backwards to arrive at the right time to sow seeds.

Today an easy way to start seeds is to sow them in moistened vermiculite (a lightweight expanded mica) or in milled sphagnum moss. Both are available at garden supply centers. Use the medium flats, cartons, pots or any container you desire. Check recommended depth for the particular seed (chart on page 26). Tiny dustlike seeds are scattered on top of the moist growing medium. Firm vermiculite around the seed by pressing gently. Label each type of seed with name, date planted and any other desired information. Water lightly and slip seed tray into a plastic bag or cover with paper. Small plastic "greenhouses" make excellent covers.

Check seed packets to see if specific light is required for germination. Follow directions.

Many gardeners today find vermiculite or milled sphagnum successful for the starting medium because of the ease in lifting out the seedlings without damage to the roots. A mixture of peat moss and vermiculite (synthetic soil mixes) is suggested for growing the seedlings to avoid loss of many seedlings due to "damping off" (weakening of the stems at soil level caused by disease organisms in garden soil and composts or standing water).

Should you decide to use compost or garden soil or to add either to the soilless mix, it will be necessary to sterilize them.

When the first true leaves of new seedlings have formed, carefully dig them out and transplant them into whatever container selected, filled with synthetic soil. Make a small hole in the container and set the seedling in it so that the leaves are ½ inch from the surface. Firmly press the mix around the roots and stem. Water carefully.

Seedlings sprout quickly under fluorescents.

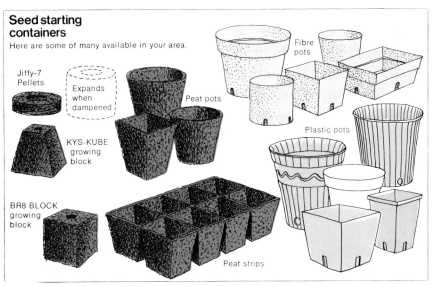

Seed starting containers

Here are some of many available in your area.

Jiffy-7 Pellets

Expands when dampened

KYS-KUBE growing block

BR8 BLOCK growing block

Peat pots

Fibre pots

Plastic pots

Peat strips

Two step method

STEP 1

Sow seeds in a small tray of vermiculite. Be sure medium is thoroughly damp before seeding. Set seeds about ¼ inch deep and about 2 inches apart. Cover seeds and water lightly. Slip tray into plastic bag and keep at about 75°. No water is necessary until after germination and then only enough to keep vermiculite damp, not soaked.

STEP 2

When the first true leaf is formed the seedlings are ready to go into 3" to 4" peat or plastic pots filled with soil mix (see text).

Pull seedling from vermiculite and set in small hole in soil mix so seed leaves (cotyledons) are about ½ inch from soil.

Press soil firmly around roots and stem.

Put pots on a tray and in a plastic bag until ready for hardening off. Wickets of coat hanger wire will keep plastic above plants.

One step method

Sow seeds, 2 at a time, directly into plastic pots, peat pots, Kys-cubes, BR8 blocks, Jiffy-7 pellets. Water thoroughly and place on a tray in a plastic bag. They'll be ready to transplant when about 6 inches high.

Growing seedlings in blocks, cubes

Seed may be sown directly in any of the pellets, blocks, or cubes (Jiffy 7 Pellets, BR8 Blocks, Kys-Kube) which have been thoroughly moistened. Place them in a warm spot according to chart recommendations (page 26). Cover blocks with paper or place in plastic bags to prevent drying out. The cubes provide all the necessary water for sprouting. After the little seedlings have appeared in the synthetic blocks, remove covers or bags. The seedlings may be nurtured in the cubes for transplanting in the garden, or the entire cube can be planted into small pots for container gardening.

Plant seedlings ready for transplanting into individual containers. Plants from seed cost only a fraction of those purchased fully grown.

Plant care for seedlings

Once the little seedlings have emerged give them as much sunlight as possible. Twelve hours a day is recommended for vegetables and herb and 5 hours for flowers. If sunlight is impossible, they will do just as well placed six inches below two 40-watt fluorescent tubes, burned 16 hours out of every 24. Special units are available in several sizes or buy the tubes and fixtures and build your own. Adjust height of the lamps as necessary during growth.

As seedlings grow they must be given room for their roots to develop. If necessary to transplant before moving outdoors, move up one pot size at a time. For those plants you intend to keep in containers for the outdoors or for moving in and out, make the transition to the large permanent pots gradually as they mature.

Transplants in transition

Young plants should not go directly from an indoor environment to the open garden. Begin to take them out for the day, gradually giving them more sunlight and return indoors at night if any danger of frost is likely.

Begin slowly to expose them to lower temperatures about two weeks before setting them out permanently. Also, gradually expose them to more sunlight.

Using seedlings

The new little plants may be transplanted directly into the ground. If using the blocks, pellets, or cubes, be sure soil covers the container completely to prevent rapid drying out of the root ball.

Pack soil down around the root ball and give extra water to the root ball in addition to regular irrigation.

HOTCAPS OR PLASTIC COVERS for young transplants are advantageous during early stages outdoors to protect from winds, frost and birds. Be sure there is ventilation to keep young plants from being cooked by heat build up. Other means of protection include cones of plastic hardware cloth attached to a stake which fits over the plant, large tin cans with each end cut-out and placed like a collar around the transplant, or use panels of wood shingles as a barrier from sun and wind.

Be creative when it comes to containers for young plants. As starters try: strawberry jars, sawed-off barrels, tubs, bushel baskets, hanging baskets. The possibilities are limitless; and don't forget the classic clay pot!

Bring your plants—vegetables, flowers or herbs—back into the house to enjoy from time-to-time. It will amaze you to watch them mature into productivity as you remember that first little leaf peeping up late last winter.

Grow foliage plants from seed

In addition to beginning vegetables and flowers for outdoor gardens, try growing house plants from seed. Seed for house plants are available from most quality seedsmen. They may be sown by the same methods described for vegetables and annuals, with bottom heat (70 to 75 degrees) added to expedite germination. Inexpensive soil heating cables are available in sizes to meet your needs. Your gardening center can secure the best type unit for your use.

SOW SEEDS SPARINGLY to eliminate bunching of seedlings which makes for poor circulation of air. Cover them the depth of their own size. Don't forget to label each planting.

CHECK SEEDS DAILY, adding water if necessary. When seedlings show move to brighter light. The first two leaves to sprout (cotyledons) nourish the stem tip and the foliage leaves which follow. Wait for foliage leaves to appear before placing in sunshine. Give seedlings the same light as you would the mature plant. Foliage plant seedlings thrive under a pair of 40-watt fluorescents as described earlier.

When seedlings begin active growth, give fertilizer biweekly with a diluted liquid solution (⅓ to ½ regular strength).

TRANSPLANT when they begin to crowd together. Start them off in individual 2¼-inch pots. Gradually move them up in pot size as necessary.

Successful house plants from seed:

African violets	*calceolaria*
begonias	*cineraria*
peperomia	cyclamen
bromeliads	gloxinia
cacti	crape-myrtlettes

Plant seedlings in whatever type container appeals to you. Use them indoors or out providing same culture as for their parents.

Perennials from seed

By following the same methods for annuals it is possible to start perennials from seed to be transplanted in the garden or potted to take outdoors as accents in your garden or patio.

Try anemone, dianthus, gaillardia, delphinium, Formosa lily, flax, Michaelmas daisy, chrysanthemum, daylily, geum, pyrethrum, bleeding-heart and blackberry-lily *(Belamcanda).*

Container grown flowering and foliage plants begun as indoor seedlings make colorful accents in the outdoor garden.

Starting flowers and vegetables from seed

Plants begun indoors in pots can remain in well-lighted window gardens or be carried outdoors as soon as the weather permits. Above is a squash, valuable for its beautiful foliage as well as harvest. The ginger in middle photo will produce deliciously fragrant blooms. Lower photo shows hanging pots of 'cherry' tomatoes over a windowsill of herbs.

Common name	Starting time* (weeks before last killing frost)	Depth to sow seeds	Temperature needed for germination
African Daisy	6-8	1/8"	65-75 degrees
Ageratum	8-12	Lightly or not at all	65-75 degrees
Amaranthus	8-12	Lightly	65-75 degrees
Asters	6-8	1/8"-1/4"	65-75 degrees
Balsam	6-8	1/8"	65-75 degrees
Begonia, Wax or Annual	16-20	do not cover	65-75 degrees
Bells of Ireland	8-10	1/8"-1/4"	35-40 degrees for 3 wks., then 65-75 degrees
Broccoli	5-7	1/2"	50-85 degrees
Browallia	12	Lightly or not at all**	65-75 degrees
Brussels Sprouts	4-6	1/2"	50-85 degrees
Cabbage	5-7	1/2"	50-85 degrees
Calendula, or Pot-Marigold	4-6	1/4"-1/2"	65-75 degrees
Carnation	8-12	Lightly	65-75 degrees
Cauliflower	5-7	1/2"	50-85 degrees
Celeriac	10-12	1/8"	50-65 degrees
Celery	10-12	1/8"	50-65 degrees
Chinese Cabbage	4-6	1/2"	50-85 degrees
Cockscomb	6-8	1/8"	65-75 degrees
Coleus	8-12	Lightly**	70-80 degrees
Collards	4-6	1/4"	50-85 degrees
Dahlia, Annual	6-8	1/4"-1/2"	65-75 degrees
Eggplant	6-9	1/4"-1/2"	65-85 degrees
Feverfew	8-12	lightly	65-75 degrees
Geranium	12-16	lightly	65-75 degrees
Gloriosa Daisy	8-12	1/8"-1/4"	65-75 degrees
Ground Cherry Husk Tomato	6	1/2"	65-85 degrees
Heliotrope	12-16	lightly**	65-75 degrees
Impatiens	12-20	lightly	70-75 degrees
Lettuce	3-5	1/4"-1/2"	50-65 degrees
Marigold	6-8	1/4"	65-75 degrees
Melons	3-4	1"	65-85 degrees
Nicotiana, or Flowering Tobacco	8-12	1/4"	65-75 degrees
Onions	8	2-3"	50-65 degrees
Peppers	6-8	1/4"	65-85 degrees
Petunia	10-12	Do not cover**	65-75 degrees
Salpiglossis	12-16	Do not cover**	65-75 degrees
Salvia, or Annual Sage	8-12	1/8"-1/4"	65-75 degrees
Snapdragon	10-12	Do not cover**	65-75 degrees
Tomatoes	5-7	1/2"	65-85 degrees
Verbena	8-12	1/8"	65-75 degrees
Vinca, or Periwinkle	12-16	1/8"	65-75 degrees

*Call the local Weather Bureau, or your County Agricultural Agent's office to learn the average date of the last killing frost in spring for your area.

**Sow seeds and press them into surface with your hand. Moisten by setting container in water or by misting surface after soil is thoroughly soaked, allow it to drain. Then put container in polyethylene bag, or cover top with clear glass, Saran wrap or wax paper held in place with rubber band. Remove covering gradually after germination is complete.

Grow primroses for a colorful garden

These beautiful plants produce a rainbow of color for container gardens beginning in early spring with some varieties blooming up into summer. There are also winter bloomers for indoors or the greenhouse. Climate of the Pacific coast area is perfect for growing primroses, but with a little care they can be used throughout the country.

Try growing your own plants from seedlings of hybrid polyanthus primroses *(P. x polyantha)* which can be purchased from West Coast specialists, or grown indoors from seed.

Contrary to recommendations of some primrose specialists, there is no need of freezing the seed before planting. As long as temperatures are not up in the 80's day and night, primrose seed can be sown. They may be sown in the fall or January to be ready for spring.

Sow the tiny seed in a moist compost of humus and sand, watering from below. Shade them with panes of glass over pots. Remove shading as seedlings begin to grow.

After the seedlings get their second or third leaves they can be transplanted into pots containing equal parts of garden loam and peat. Mix a cup of any commercial fertilizer with each bushel of soil mixture.

Keep cool, with night temperatures at 50 degrees and water thoroughly. Best results occur when they can be placed in a cold frame as soon as weather permits. In mild climates they can go directly outdoors.

Move to their garden spot in early spring. Use in containers as desired. The pots underneath the tree shown on page 22 provide bed of instant color. Keep them moist, fertilized and cool. Watch for slugs and snails and use bait for them.

P. sinensis (Chinese primrose), *P. malacoides* (fairy primrose) and *P. obconica,* all Asiatic in origin, bloom in winter. They can be grown as above and summered outdoors in cold frames for prolific fall and winter blooms in the greenhouse or interior spaces where night temperatures can be lowered to 50 degrees.

Primroses have few rivals for color in a late winter garden in mild climates or an early spring garden elsewhere.

Mexican clay chicken sprouts ruffly feathers of parsley.

Scented geraniums come in many delicious fragrances. Here are plants in lemon, rose, pineapple, nutmeg and apple.

A handcrafted crate makes a good looking planter for a kitchen garden of mixed herbs. Keep in a sunny indoor spot or outdoors. It's easy to carry through the kitchen door.

Begin herbs indoors

Nothing sparks good cooking like the use of freshly-picked herbs. These plants are treasured because of their fragrant, useful foliage, or in some cases, flowers.

Beware of some of the commercially packaged herb gardens which direct you to grow the seed in terrariums or enclosed containers, as warned on page 33. Herbs thrive best in fresh air and sunshine. A temperature range of 50° to 75° is needed for a healthy herb harvest. Grow them in a sunny kitchen window or just outside the kitchen door for easy access.

Grow herbs from seed in the same methods described for vegetables or purchase seedlings from plant markets. When the seedlings are ready for transplanting, pot in a soil mix of equal parts garden loam, sand, well-rotted and pulverized manure and peat moss or leaf mold. Or use commercial houseplant pre-mixed soil. Keep herbs labeled always.

Be gentle with pest controls for herbs that are to be eaten. Most gardeners simply wash leaves in a mild solution of liquid soap and water.

The herbs can remain indoors in a permanent herb garden or be summered outdoors in all types of containers, window boxes, or transplanted to the garden. Foliage may be severely pruned when transferring outdoors to produce healthy, new growth. Repot into new soil at the end of summer and bring back to the window garden before heat is turned on in the house.

Wash foliage once a week while indoors to clean and aid growth. Build up humidity by placing pots on a tray of moist pebbles. Rotate the pots weekly toward sunlight for uniform growth. Pinch out growing tips to make plant bushier. Provide fresh air as often as possible.

Try these herbs in hanging baskets: borage, mints, rosemary, tarragon and thyme.

Herbs thrive under fluorescent lighting, enabling people everywhere to have a year-round supply of garden-fresh herbs. (See page 9).

Over abundance of herbs can be dried for culinary uses. The best method is quick-drying by spreading leaves on a wire mesh rack in a slow oven for a few minutes. Also, they can be tied in bunches and hung to dry in a clean, shaded place with fresh air circulation.

Herb planting directions

Name	Method of starting	Starting Time
Anise	Seeds	Spring or fall
Basil, sweet	Seeds	Fall or spring
Bay, sweet	Buy young plants	Early fall
Borage	Buy young plants	Late summer
Carraway	Seeds	Spring or fall
Chamomile	Buy young plants	Late summer
Chervil	Seeds	Anytime
Chives	From small clumps	Anytime
Coriander	Seeds	Summer or fall
Dill	Seeds	Late summer or early fall
Fennel	Seeds	Summer or fall
Garden cress	Seeds (darkness)	Anytime
Horehound	Seeds	Spring
Lemon Balm	Seeds or Buy young plants	Anytime or fall
Lemon-verbena	Buy young plants	Fall
Marjoram, sweet	Seeds	Anytime
Mints	Buy young plants	Spring or fall
Parsley	Seeds, soak 24 hours or Buy young plants	Spring or fall
Rosemary	Buy young plants	Spring or fall
Sage	Buy young plants	Spring or fall
Savory	Buy young plants	Spring or fall
Scented geraniums	Buy young plants	Spring or fall
Tarragon	Buy young plants	Spring or fall
Thyme	Buy young plants	Spring or fall

Here are a few uses of flowering annuals, vegetables and herbs begun from seed indoors in winter and placed outside as climate permits. Top left, elegant *delphinium* stands at attention in classic clay pots. Top right shows a strawberry jar overflowing with colorful pansies. Mixed annuals are planted in the strawberry jar and pots in the photo underneath. The middle photo on the right shows a ceramic pot of pansies. The large picture features an impatiens cushioned on a carpet of baby's tears. In the bottom photos, reading left to right, we see young lettuce leaves in a hand-thrown West Indian pot, vividly colored annuals cascading from a hanging patio basket, and lastly, a stoneware pot of lemon scented geranium. Any of these plants can thrive outdoors through warm weather or be carried inside for showy accents whenever desired.

How to rescue the last flowers of Summer

Flowers you can save from frost and grow inside. How to do it and what to realistically expect from them.

Unless you live where Jack Frost brings a sudden and final end to the gardening season, it is hard to understand the sad, desperate feeling this brings to Northern gardeners. Total surrender is not necessary, however. There are many tender perennial flowers which we grow outdoors in warm weather as annuals which can be brought inside before frost for an extended flowering season. In a sunny window, under fluorescent lights or in a home greenhouse, some will keep blooming indefinitely. For others this bringing inside is merely to capture a few more flowers before the plant dies. And for some it is a holding operation meant to keep the plant alive, but not in active growth, until the following spring or summer when once again it can be put outdoors.

Moving from outdoors to indoors

If the plant you want to save is already growing in a pot or hanging basket of a size convenient to bring inside, the procedure is simple. Set the plant up on a bench or table where you can really see it. Wipe the container clean. Then clip off every yellowed leaf, spent flower and seed pod. If the plant is too large for the space you have inside, study the branch structure and cut back; your aim is to retain a pleasing overall shape with as many healthy leaves and flower buds as possible at the same time you reduce the overall size of the plant.

Check the plant for pests and treat with recommended pesticides according to directions before bringing it indoors. Containers of soil brought in from outdoors may also contain gnats, earthworms and sowbugs—of no earth-shaking consequence, but not exactly the most charming indoor visitors. To eradicate, drench the soil with malathion (mix ½ teaspoon 50 percent emulsifiable concentrate in 1 quart of water) before bringing plants indoors. Sometimes it is necessary to repeat the procedure.

If both plant and container are too large to bring inside, then potting down is in order. This procedure is illustrated in the step-by-step photographs below.

Digging plants from the garden

Plants growing directly in the ground, whether in beds or in large planters, require careful transplanting, and even so they will suffer more shock than those simply transferred in pots from outdoors to indoors. The best time to dig and pot up is two or three weeks before frost is expected. This allows for a period of recuperation outdoors in a shady, moist spot before the final move indoors. Depending on the size of the plant you want to dig and pot up, use either a sturdy trowel or a sharpshooter spade. If the soil is dry, apply water a day or two before digging. This will make your work easier and will also save root damage. From the moment you dig up the plant with a good chunk of earth surrounding the root system, the

Petunias and wax begonias are among the outdoor summer flowers that can be brought indoors for an extended season.

procedure is the same as for potting down, illustrated below.

Flowers you can save

Annual or tender perennial flowers that send up sturdy new basal growth whenever the tops are cut back are the best to save. These include wax or semperflorens begonia, petunia and flowering tobacco (nicotiana). Snapdragon also will send up basal

When flowering plants have grown all summer outdoors they are usually too large to bring inside as they are. It seems a shame to let frost end their productivity. Here's a step-by-step series of how to pot down to a size for indoors that will be easy to handle and increase blooming. **A.** *This large geranium has provided outdoor blooms all summer long. Let's rescue it for winter bloom.* **B.** *Remove the plant from its pot. Note the rootbound condition.* **C.** *Carefully loosen soil around the roots with hands in preparation for repotting.*

Why give up these beautiful blooms when frost comes? They can be prepared to bring indoors for enjoyment for a few more weeks or even months in some cases. Petunias (left) continue to grow well indoors. Heliotrope (top center) and impatiens (right) are very successful when transplanted carefully and kept moist. Browallia and petunias on the porch are ready for the indoor transition.

growth after cutting back, but it is definitely a cool-weather plant, suited only to a moist, airy, cool greenhouse or sun porch. With careful transplanting and attention to keeping the soil moist afterwards, you can have success saving healthy, flowering plants of geranium, heliotrope, ageratum, lobelia, French marigold, lantana, impatiens, torenia, browallia, sage (salvia), sweet-alyssum and verbena.

Annual phlox, zinnia, China-aster or tall African or hybrid marigolds are difficult indoors. All of these need some sunlight in fall and winter in order to continue flowering. Since they will have already been blooming for several months, it is too much to expect them to continue indefinitely, but if you keep the soil moist, feed every two weeks with a liquid houseplant food, and keep all spent blooms clipped off, they will extend summer for weeks. Plants of this type are ideal to fill a new greenhouse while you are collecting and starting permanent seeds, cuttings and bulbs.

While you are rescuing these flowers from frost, remember also to bring in tender bulbs such as caladium, achimenes, tuberous begonia and amaryllis. You can also pot up, trim and keep such herbs as borage, lemon-verbena, sweet basil, marjoram, parsley and scented-leaf geraniums.

D. *Soil has been removed from long roots of the geranium.* **E.** *With sharp shears cut the roots approximately in half. This will encourage new growth after repotting.* **F.** *Select a pot about one half the size of the original. Follow potting procedures outlined on pages 14 through 15.* **G.** *With pruning shears cut back the plant to about one half its original size. Water well and apply fertilizer. It is good to do this several weeks before frost so the plants will have time to adjust before placing in a sunny indoor location.*

Little gardens anyone can grow

Ideas for thimbles,
bottles, bowls,
dishes and terrariums

You don't have to have a plot of ground or a sunny window to grow a garden. In fact, you don't even have to be ambulatory. The answer lies in miniature plants and proportionately small containers. Complete gardens you can hold in your hands represent the ultimate in gardening pleasure. The only way you can plant and care for them is to be in intimate personal contact. You smell the goodness of moist earth and growing plants. You see the slightest changes, every new leaf, every furling bud.

Landscaping in miniature

When you place several or many different plants in one container you are creating a landscape effect. This is true whether you are working in a fish tank, a bubble bowl or brandy snifter, in a bottle or a shallow cast-iron or ceramic bonsai tray.

◊

A Victorian era conservatory in miniature combines moisture-loving tropicals of several kinds.

Depending on your personal likes, the plants you have available, the container and where you want your landscape to grow, you can create the effect of a woodland dell, the desert, or a rocky or sandy coastline. You can also do your planting in the manner of a garden you have visited or seen pictured in Japan, England, the Alps, or you can arrange the plants in rows, representing a neatly organized nursery.

Terrarium plantings

The most common misconception about terrariums is that they require no care and will thrive just anywhere you'd like a little spot of nature around the house. Do not be misled. A terrarium is a living microcosm of nature.

Collections of cacti and other succulents need a few hours of direct sun in order to stay shapely. Other plants need bright, indirect light and most will do better with some direct sun, especially early in the morning or in late afternoon. The same as bottle gardens, terrariums of all kinds grow perfectly in a fluorescent-light garden. They also need water from time to time, and routine maintenance to remove spent growth and to keep rampant growers compact. A pre-planted terrarium that appears to be stuffed with plants is not a good investment, and avoid any kind of terrarium kit for growing herbs. Herbs make fine pot plants for a sunny window or fluorescent-light garden, but they need fresh, circulating air and perfect drainage. They are not terrarium material.

If there is space in your terrarium, you can add a shallow container of water to serve as a pond. Sometimes a little circle or oval mirror is used to represent water, but the real thing is nicer, especially when creepers like selaginella grow around naturally, like full-scale English ivy outdoors.

Another interesting effect with a fairly tall, glass terrarium container is to add several undulating layers of different colored sand, pebbles, soil, charcoal chips and even pulverized pieces of broken clay pot. This technique gives the effect of the geological layers of the earth in cross section.

AIR-BORNE TERRARIUMS. Mostly we think of terrariums as tabletop decorations, but they can also be suspended from ceiling hooks or wall brackets. Macramé holders are excellent, and have a natural appearance in keeping with a terrarium. There are also leaded glass terrarium containers on the market, designed

for hanging. Some of these are beautifully conceived, quite like the ornate Wardian cases of the Victorian era. Remember, however, when you select any glass container to hold plants they will do best if the glass is clear, not tinted. Water-cooler jugs make great bottle gardens, for example, but for best results use only the clear, not the blue- or green-tinted kinds.

Top is removed from an octagonal redwood frame terrarium for occasional ventilation.

Planting basics

Most containers used for this kind of gardening have no drainage holes. To help keep the growing medium in good health, and therefore sweet-smelling and conducive to good growth, first line the bottom of the container with a half inch of charcoal chips. You'll find these in bags wherever indoor plants and supplies are sold. Next add a minimum of 1 inch potting soil. It's easiest to use a commercially prepared medium labeled "for terrarium plantings." It is true that not all of these are exactly what they're cracked up to be. The most common complaint is that they are too dense, too rich, too moisture-retentive. This sounds like three faults, but they are all inter-relating. If you open up a bag of terrarium soil and find it appears to be any of these things, add some vermiculite or perlite. Any of the soilless mixtures are fine for miniature landscapes (see page 10).

If you are planting a desertscape, using only cacti and other succulents that grow naturally in sandy, dry places, add extra sand, grit or perlite to terrarium soil. Actually, most of these are not terribly particular about the growing medium. Unless you water with a very heavy hand there should be no problem.

A French storage jar holds a miniature landscape featuring small leaf ivy.

Depending on the container depth you can add more than 1 inch of growing medium, but that is the minimum. If your landscape will be flat, like the Texas prairie, then level off the surface and proceed with

planting. If you want rolling hills, **move** the earth around until you have the effect that pleases. When all plants are in place, you can do the final shaping of the terrain. If you want a rocky or mountainous effect, use a piece of lightweight stone such as Featherock; some nurseries sell this, or check in your Yellow Pages under "Stone—Natural."

If your little landscape is to be a woodland scene, look for a piece of partially decayed wood— like a rotting log in miniature. If a Lilliputian sea-coast is your dream, search for suitably small, interesting pieces of driftwood.

Plants for little landscapes

In the accompanying photographs you will find 12 plants suggested for moist shade, 12 for dry sun. The best plants for miniature gardens are those that naturally grow and stay small. Next best are kinds that grow slowly, although they will eventually outgrow a mini landscape.

In a bottle or terrarium with a cover, these plants are excellent: Small ferns such as *Polystichum tsus-sinense*, *Pellaea rotundifolia* and babies of *Asplenium bulbiferum* and *A. vivi-*

Filtered natural light silhouettes the terrain in a bubble jar.

parum. Sinningia pusilla and other miniature gloxinias. Any selaginella or club moss. Strawberry-geranium, either *Saxifraga stolonifera* or its variegated form (which needs more coolness ideally). Small cryptanthus or earth stars. Miniature rex begonias. Fittonia. Episcia. *Gesneria cuneifolia* and its hybrid 'Lemon Drop'—both are nearly everblooming.

For a terrarium in open air but not much sun you can grow almost any of the plants previously suggested, and also seedlings or rooted cuttings of virtually any shade plant.

COLLECTION FOR MOIST, SHADED GARDEN: *(Left to right)* Back row: Peperomia rotundifolia, Maranta kerchoveana *(prayer plant)*, Hedera helix scutifolia *(ivy)* and Cryptanthus acaulis *(earth stars)*. Middle row: Saxifraga stolonifera *(strawberry geranium)*, Pilea nummulariifolia *(creeping charlie)*, Cryptanthus bromelioides *and* Chamaedorea elegans *(Neanthe bella palm)*. Front row: Selaginella kraussiana brownii *(clubmoss)*, Cryptanthus *(earth stars)*, Asplenium palmatum *and* Adiantum raddianum *(maidenhair fern)*.

Cacti and other succulents are used quite effectively in bowl gardens. Bowls or dishes must have drainage holes or added layers of charcoal or gravel. The small desertscapes can take many forms, limited only to your imagination. Use tiny pieces of driftwood, sand or gravel to complete your scene. Place in good light and follow cultural directions for the species.

COLLECTION FOR A DRY, SUNNY GARDEN: *(Left to right) Back row:* Acanthocalycium violaceum, Crassula punctulata, Euphorbia aeruginosa *and* Sempervivum cilitana. *Middle row:* Astrophytum myriostigma, Crassula punctulata, Echeveria valentine *and* Echeveria harmoil. *Front row:* Sedum hakonense, Echinopsis cereitormsis, Mammillaria spinosissima *and* Villadia batesi. *Remember to provide lean, gritty growing medium and plenty of good, quick drainage. Most other succulents need less sunlight than cacti.*

Bottle planting

Bowls, dishes, brandy snifters and fish tanks are easy to plant and maintain because you can reach your hands into them. Small-necked bottles are quite another thing. Like switching on the lights when you know the electricity is off, you will find yourself expecting to use your hands to assist in planting when actually you will have to use long-handled tools.

To place charcoal chips and the growing medium in a bottle, you can fashion a fairly effective funnel from a rolled piece of newspaper. This will help keep particles of soil off the inside walls of the bottle. To move the soil around and shape the terrain you can use a piece of slender bamboo stake with a half-teaspoon measuring spoon taped on the end.

When you are ready to "bottle" your plants, gently remove most of the soil from the roots. Then drop each plant through the neck, and, using your bamboo-spoon-spade, coax it into the right position and cover the roots with soil.

Bottle planting requires the patience of Job, but it is immensely satisfying. You may easily spend an entire evening or lazy afternoon planting one bottle garden. After the plants are in place, a final mulch or ground carpeting of green woods moss or florists sheet moss will give your landscape a nice finishing touch. Then use a mister of clean water to settle the roots and remove particles of soil from the leaves and sides of the bottle. Be careful not to add too much water, however, or you will have a floating garden. Before you add any plant to a bottle, inspect it carefully to be sure it is host to no insects.

Bottle gardens do best in bright but not direct sunlight. If sun shines directly on the bottle for more than an hour or two the plants are likely to be cooked. Bottle gardens do superbly well under two fluorescent tubes, one Cool White, one Warm White, either 20- or 40-watt, burned 12 to 14 hours out of every 24. If the soil in your bottle garden appears to be dry, or if the plants appear lackluster, or if no moisture droplets form inside, add a little water. To remove yellowing leaves, spent flowers, or excess growth, tape a single-edge razor blade to a piece of slender bamboo, and use it as your cutting tool. You can remove clippings with a mechanic's pick-up tool(sold at automobile parts supply houses), or by using two pieces of bamboo stake, chopstick fashion. It is important that you remove dying leaves and flowers, otherwise they will rot.

Thimble size gardens

Growing miniature plants in tiny containers is the height of Lilliputian gardening. It is possible to have living, thriving, even flowering plants in dollhouse dishes, caps of toothpaste, 1¼ -inch plastic pots, in bottle lids and even in thimbles. If you like to pamper plants, here is your chance. The soil in thumb-size containers dries out quickly. Check it in the morning, at noon if possible, and again in the evening. Soil that is nicely damp in the morning may be parched by nightfall. Apply water with an eyedropper or, when possible, by immersing the pot until the growing medium and roots are well moistened.

Thimble planting

When you plant a thimble-size container, leave ⅛ inch of space at the top to allow room for watering. Some growers place a little bit of sand in the bottom of thimblelike pots, but this is usually not necessary; the problem is keeping the soil uniformly moist at all times, not keeping it drier.

Use fine-textured or sifted potting soil, and once every two or three weeks apply a few drops of very dilute liquid house-plant food (mix it at one-fourth the strength recommended on the container for standard-size pot plants). To keep some of them to the right proportions, careful pinching or pruning will be needed. You can use a pair of manicuring scissors as your pruning shears. By this technique, a seed of an orange or lemon planted in a thimble

Miniature plants in thimble sized clay pots suitable for miniature landscapes or gardening in tiny planters.

may, without transplanting, be grown in it for up to three years.

SEEDLINGS OF MOST CACTI and other succulents are delightful for this form of gardening. They have interesting shapes, unusual textures, appealing colors and most of them tolerate considerable drouth and heat. Other plants to grow in tiny containers include *Acorus gramineus pusillus,* rooted tip cuttings of rosary vine (*Ceropegia woodii),* species of *Conophytum,* miniature creeping fig (*Ficus repens pumila),* miniature varieties of English ivy ('Itsy Bitsy' for example), rooted tip cuttings of 'Tom Thumb' kalanchoe, sweet alyssum seedlings, tip cuttings of *Philodendron sodiroi,* tiny offsets of sedum, and miniature gloxinias and African violets. In addition you can use seedlings or little offshoots from virtually any of the plants suggested in the following text and picture captions.

Other little plants

Where living quarters are cramped, true miniature plants are the answer. Most nearly perfect are the miniature gloxinias. The first of these to gain popularity was *Sinningia pusilla,* then its relative, *S. concinna.* Now there are several dozen named hybrids derived from these. A mature plant of any of them can be cupped in a child's hand. The major breeder and source for them is Michael Kartuz, 92 Chestnut Street, Wilmington, Massachusetts 01887. Miniature African violets are only slightly larger. Specialists include Annalee Violetry, 29-50 214th Place, Bayside, New York 11360; Champion's African Violets, 8848 Van Hoesen Road, Clay, New York 13041; Lyndon Lyon, 14 Mutchler Street, Dolgeville, New York 13329; and Mary-Ray Violets, 5007 Terry Drive, Alton, Illinois 62002. For miniature begonias, Kartuz is also the chief supplier. For miniature geraniums and English ivies, write to Merry Gardens, Camden, Maine 04843. If you have the collector spirit, look into miniature orchids—there are literally thousands. Some of the best are available from Alberts & Merkel, Box 537, Boynton Beach, Florida 33435; Fennell Orchid Company, 26715 S.W. 157th Avenue, Homestead, Florida 33030; and Fred A. Stewart, Inc., 1212 East Las Tunas Drive, San Gabriel, California 91778.

For a complete guide to miniature gardening, see *Little Plants for Small Spaces,* by Elvin McDonald (Popular Library, New York; $1.50).

How to plant a bottle garden

1. Clean and polish bottle with moist paper towel held in wooden tongs. Dampen towel with window-cleaning spray to remove stains. Let dry before planting.

2. Add 1 inch layers of sand and charcoal chips—then a few inches of potting soil using a funnel and paper tube extension to help keep dust down and off sides of bottle.

3. Roll larger, leafy plants in paper cylinder to slip them through the neck without damage.

4. Use wooden tongs to lower small plants through the neck and to maneuver all plants into position.

5. A spoon taped to a stick is great for digging planting holes, positioning plants, covering roots, and shaping the terrain.

6. A spool on a stick can be used to tamp and firm soil.

7. Shaping and pruning can be done with a razor blade taped to a stick. Pick up prunings with tongs.

8. Use a bulb syringe to wash sides of glass, water roots into place and settle soil. Use it dry to blow dust and soil particles off glass or leaves.

You don't have to be rich to have a greenhouse

Install low-cost prefabs with a wrench and screwdriver or dig sun-heated pits.

Energy from the sun is utilized to heat this sunken greenhouse. Even in cold winter climates supplementary heating is unnecessary, but can be added for plants that enjoy warmth. Construction and upkeep costs are very low.

In these days of high building costs, it may surprise you to learn that prices for prefabricated home greenhouses have remained stable at very little more than they were ten years ago. In fact, they are such a good buy that many people are using them to add on a room to the house where plants can surround family activities.

You can also build a greenhouse from scratch, using rot-resistant redwood or cypress for the frame, and glass, heavy-duty polyethylene plastic or fiber glass for the cover. The initial investment need not be large, but in cold climates the continuing expense of heating is of concern, especially when fuel may be in short supply. One answer is to attach the greenhouse to your dwelling, with windows or doors that open into it. In many situations, this allows the existing home heating system to also heat the greenhouse at relatively low cost. In the recent fuel shortage many private as well as commercial growers lowered winter temperatures in their greenhouses. Although growth of warmth-loving tropicals was slowed, in general there seemed to be no bad effects.

Mrs. Kathryn Taylor has enjoyed her sun-heated pit greenhouse for nearly 40 years.

Sun-heated pit greenhouses

Another way to beat the fuel problem is to let the sun do your greenhouse heating. This is not a new idea by any means. In the 19th and early 20th centuries large pits of this type were fairly common, especially on up-North estates where great numbers of frost-tender tropical trees, shrubs and bulbs were wintered over in this way. By this approach the lower half of the greenhouse is dug into the ground and the half of the roof span facing north is boxed in, shingled and heavily insulated. The other half of the span, facing south, is glazed in glass and covered at night and on cloudy, cold days with thick, heavy mats of straw or old carpeting. In more recent years feather-weight sheets of plastic foam have proved to be efficient and much more easily handled insulating mats.

The adaptation of estate-sized sun-heated pits for home gardeners is attributed to Mr. and Mrs. Lucien B. Taylor whose 1937 model pit is shown in the photographs here. After nearly 40 years the structure is still sound and a constant source of pleasure for the Taylors. In a climate where winter temperatures sometimes dip to zero, they have not found supplementary heating necessary. Other pits in their neighborhood are

operated in the same fashion, though some have auxiliary electric heat to boost temperatures for plants that need more winter warmth.

Sun-heated pits make an ideal place for growing camellias, acacias, all kinds of glorious primroses, sweet-scented English violets, a host of fascinating alpine plants and for forcing tulips, daffodils, hyacinths, crocus and other bulbs all winter long. Scented-leaf geraniums do well, along with all of the herbs commonly used in cooking. Detailed information about building and running a sun-heated pit may be found in Mrs. Taylor's book, which she wrote along with Edith Gregg, called *Winter Flowers in the Sun-Heated Pit* (published by Scribner's, New York).

Prefab greenhouse units are available to fit almost any type window. Or you can construct your own low-cost design.

Window greenhouses

Where space or budget does not permit, a window greenhouse may be the answer. These are available as prefabricated units in a wide range of sizes. You can also buy automatic ventilators and heating units for these. Anyone the least bit handy with a saw and hammer can build a serviceable window greenhouse, using redwood or cypress and glass, polyethylene or fiber glass as the covering material.

Especially for starting seeds and cuttings in the spring, you can fashion polyethylene-covered wooden frames to place over basement window openings. Cool nighttime temperatures help maintain stocky, compact growth and transplants that do well later in the garden.

Before you begin construction of any kind of home greenhouse, check local building restrictions. In some communities greenhouses are permitted only if attached to the dwelling. City codes are especially tricky when greenhouse construction involves building on a roof or terrace, but if it's feasible at all a good architect can help you cut the red tape.

Whether you build from scratch or go the prefabricated way, it is possible to have a greenhouse for what a console color TV costs.

When to plant what for a flowering greenhouse

(Note: This schedule is designed for a home greenhouse maintained in the winter months at moderate temperatures: 50 to 60° at night, with a daytime rise of 10 to 15°.)

January. *Divide/repot* geraniums, orchids. *Make cuttings* of ageratum, beloperone, campanula, carnation, crassula, crossandra and geranium. *Plant bulbs* of yellow and pink calla-lilies. *Plant seeds* of calendula, candytuft, centaurea, felicia, gerbera, godetia, gypsophila, impatiens, kalanchoe, lobelia, marigold, nierembergia, petunia, salpiglossis, schizanthus, snapdragon, solanum, sweet alyssum, sweet pea and ursinia.

February. *Divide/repot* abutilon, agapanthus, orchids, strelitzia and tulbaghia. *Make cuttings* of acalypha, ageratum, allamanda, beloperone, campanula, crossandra, dipladenia, dusty miller, lantana and tibouchina. *Plant bulbs* of agapanthus and yellow and pink calla-lilies. *Plant seeds* of ageratum, felicia, gerbera, gypsophila, kalanchoe, lobelia, nierembergia, petunia, schizanthus, snapdragon, solanum and verbena.

March. *Divide/repot* abutilon, agapanthus, ardisia, beloperone, camellia, capsicum, haemanthus, orchids and strelitzia. *Make cuttings* of aphelandra, ardisia, beloperone, bouvardia, coleus, crassula, crossandra, dipaldenia, echeveria, geranium, Chinese

hibiscus, hoya, ixora, jasmine, lantana, oleander, passiflora, salvia, stephanotis, stevia and tibouchina. *Plant bulbs* of achimenes and haemanthus. *Plant seeds* of abutilon, acacia, ardisia, azalea, browallia, camellia, clivia, felicia, freesia, gypsophila, kalanchoe, oleander, primrose, smithiantha and solanum.

April. *Divide/repot* abutilon ardisia, camellia, haemanthus, orchids and strelitzia. *Make cuttings* of aphelandra, ardisia, beloperone, bougainvillea, bouvardia, chrysanthemum, crassula, crossandra, dipladenia, echeveria, euphorbia, geranium, Chinese hibiscus, hoya, hydrangea, ixora, jasmine, lantana, marguerite, oleander, passiflora, pentas, salvia, stephanotis, stevia and tibouchina. *Plant bulbs* of achimenes and gladiolus. *Plant seeds* of abutilon, acacia, anemone, ardisia, China-aster, browallia, capsicum, cineraria, clivia, felicia, gypsophila, kalanchoe, oleander, primrose, smithiantha and solanum.

May. *Divide/repot* abutilon, ardisia, camellia, haemanthus and orchids. *Make cuttings* of aphelandra, ardisia, beloperone, bougainvillea, bouvardia, chrysanthemum, citrus, crassula, crossandra, echeveria, euphorbia, felicia, geranium, Chinese hibiscus, hoya, ixora, marguerite, oleander, osmanthus, passiflora, salvia, stephanotis, stevia and tibouchina. *Plant seeds* of abutilon, anemone, ardisia, browallia, camellia, cineraria, clivia, coleus, exacum, felicia, gazania, gypsophila, impatiens, kalanchoe, myosotis, oleander, primrose, salvia and smithiantha.

June. *Divide/repot* acacia and orchids. *Make cuttings* of acacia, azalea, beloperone, bougainvillea, chrysanthemum, citrus, clematis, crassula, echeveria, euphorbia, felicia, geranium, Chinese hibiscus, hoya, marguerite, oleander, osmanthus, passiflora, punica, salvia and tibouchina. *Plant seeds* of anemone, browallia, calceolaria, cineraria, coleus, cyclamen, didiscus, exacum, felicia, gazania, gypsophila, heliotrope, impatiens, kalanchoe, myosotis, oleander, nicotiana, petunia, primrose, salvia, smithiantha and ursinia.

July. *Divide/repot* orchids. *Make cuttings* of acacia, azalea, beloperone, citrus, clematis, coleus, crassula, crossandra, euphorbia, fuchsia,

geranium, heliotrope, Chinese hibiscus, impatiens, oleander, osmanthus, passiflora, petunia, punica and salvia. *Plant seeds* of calendula, coleus, cyclamen, didiscus, dimorphotheca, felicia, gypsophila, impatiens, kalanchoe, myosotis, oleander, nicotiana, petunia, primrose, salvia, snapdragon, stock, sweet alyssum and ursinia.

August. *Divide/repot* orchids and veltheimia. *Make cuttings* of azalea, beloperone, camellia, coleus, crassula, crossandra, fuchsia, geranium, impatiens, oleander and passiflora. *Plant bulbs* of cyrtanthus, freesia, lachenalia and oxalis. *Plant seeds* of China-aster, bellis, calendula, centaurea, celosia, cineraria, coleus, cyclamen, didiscus, dimorphotheca, gypsophila, marigold, nasturtium, oleander, nicotiana, Phlox drummondi, primrose, salvia, schizanthus, snapdragon, stock and sweet alyssum.

September. *Divide/repot* orchids, ornithogalum, primrose and veltheimia. *Make cuttings* of abutilon, azalea, beloperone, crassula, crossandra, jasmine, lantana and petunia. *Plant bulbs* of anemone, babiana, calla-lily (white), crocus, cyrtanthus, daffodil, hyacinth, Dutch iris, ixia, lachenalia, paperwhite narcissus, ornithogalum and veltheimia. *Plant seeds* of China-aster, calceolaria, centaurea, cineraria, clarkia, didiscus, godetia, gypsophila, marigold, nasturtium, Phlox drummondi, salpiglossis, salvia, schizanthus, snapdragon and ursinia.

October. *Divide/repot* cyrtanthus, orchids and ornithogalum. *Make cuttings* of abutilon, azalea, beloperone, crassula, crossandra and lantana. *Plant bulbs* of crocus, cyrtanthus, daffodil, hyacinth, ixia, narcissus and tulip. *Plant seeds* of China-aster, calendula, cineraria, godetia, salpiglossis, stock and ursinia.

November. *Divide/repot* cyrtanthus, orchids and ornithogalum. *Make cuttings* of azalea, beloperone, crassula and crossandra. *Plant bulbs* of crocus, daffodil, hyacinth, ixia and tulip. *Plant seeds* of clarkia and godetia.

December. *Divide/repot* orchids. *Make cuttings* of beloperone, crassula and crossandra. *Plant bulbs* of amaryllis. *Plant seeds* of candytuft, godetia, nierembergia and petunia (especially double grandifloras).

Home greenhouse basics

Whether you buy a prefabricated greenhouse, or build your own even-span, lean-to or sun-heated pit, be sure you make it large enough. The universal complaint of home green-house owners is that they built too small. Yet, when well managed, it is truly amazing what can be cultivated in a space measuring 6 by 9 feet. The size you select will depend on what you can afford, the space you have and what you want to grow.

In cold winter climates greenhouses need full sun. Deciduous trees nearby are fine since they admit winter sun but give shade in summer. Toward the South you can site the greenhouse facing east or west and still grow sun-loving plants in the winter.

Several easily constructed greenhouses using inexpensive materials.

A greenhouse provides the home gardener with much pleasure and year-round flowers, fruiting trees, vegetables and all types of foliage plants, vines and shrubs.

A geodesic dome prefabricated greenhouse unit constructed of redwood is available from commercial greenhouse distributors at prices beginning under $100.

If you wish to use the greenhouse in summer, some means of cooling will be necessary. Shade in the form of bamboo blinds, lath, venetian blinds or Lumite saran cloth will help, but you will also need a circulating fan pulling outside air through wet aspen pads and exhausting the hot air. Automatic ventilators that open and shut windows for temperature control are almost a requisite even in the winter.

Cool or alpine greenhouses maintained with winter nighttime temperatures between 40 and 50° are the least expensive to maintain, and they also require somewhat less care since the plants do not grow so rapidly and the coolness is less conducive to pests and diseases.

For general growing a moderate greenhouse is ideal. With a winter nighttime minimum temperature range of 50 to 60°, almost all plants can be cultivated. What you do is locate cold and hot microclimates within the greenhouse and use these to accom-modate plants accordingly. Because a moderate greenhouse can cover such a wide variety of plants, our schedule of when to plant what for a flowering greenhouse (page 40) is based on this plan. Wintertime day temperatures can rise 10 to 15° or so in order to maintain sturdy, constant growth.

Warm greenhouses are for true tropicals, for example many orchids, gesneriads, bromeliads, philoden-drons and anthuriums. Where winter cold is extreme, such a structure will be costly to heat, but then who can say it isn't worth it on a windy, snowy, subzero morning when you step into the fragrance and warmth of your tropical paradise?

Whatever happened to Winter?

The May-in-December pleasures of fooling Mother Nature into giving early blooms

One rewarding aspect of indoor gardening is to persuade plants to bloom out of season. By duplicating—but shortening—the stages bulbs go through in your garden, you can have tulips, daffodils and hyacinths blooming in the house in areas where the wind drifts snow outside. Warmer climate dwellers also enjoy these spring bulbs ahead of time.

Besides bulbs to force, there are some hardy perennials that respond to this treatment—hosta, astilbe, bleeding-heart and lily-of-the-valley.

There are annual flowers, too, for a sunny indoor garden, plus branches of favorite flowering shrubs.

How to force hardy bulbs

It's easy to force tulips, daffodils, ornithogalum, hyacinths and the little bulbs—crocuses, snowdrops and grape-hyacinths—to bloom indoors ahead of their normal time outdoors. Grow them as Christmas gifts for friends. Start with the largest size bulbs obtainable. Read the catalogs carefully to select those varieties

Bulbs for colorful winter forcing include (clockwise, beginning top left) crocus, daffodils, ornithogalum, hyacinth, babiana tubergens, streptattens and narcissus.

the firm recommends for forcing or, buy the ones we list. Order by September so the bulbs will be delivered in early fall. Then follow these steps:

SOIL MIXTURE for bulbs can be made up of equal parts soil, sand and peat moss. To each 5-inch pot of this mix, add a teaspoon of bone meal. If you don't want the bother of mixing soil, buy a soilless medium. Used in large quantities, these get to be costly; for how to mix your own soilless medium, see page 11.

POT SIZE depends on the kind and quantity of bulbs. One large daffodil or tulip bulb can be planted in a 4- or 5-inch pot in which three crocuses or other smaller bulbs would fit. For six tulips, daffodils or hyacinths, you'll need a 6- to 10-inch pot. When you plant these large bulbs, cover the tops of tulips and hyacinths with a ½ inch of soil. Don't try to cover the necks of daffodils—just the fattened portion of the bulb. Cover the smaller bulbs, like crocuses, with a ½ inch of soil. Then water thoroughly. It is also possible to purchase pre-planted containers of bulbs which are conditioned to begin the forcing process.

BULBS NEED A PERIOD OF COOLNESS after potting so that they can form a vigorous root system. Without a potful of roots, they cannot bloom prolifically later on. Tradition has it that you will bury these pots of bulbs in a bed of cinders outdoors in a coldframe, leaving them there until at least New Year's Day (except some pre-conditioned bulbs which will bloom for Christmas). This system is impractical for most of us today, and besides, there are easier ways to accomplish the same thing. Find a cool, frost-free place where bulbs can be forced. A garage attached to the house, but not heated is a good place for bulbs to form roots. A cool attic, or a cool basement also will do. We use a window in the cold room of our basement. A temperature range of 35° to 55° will promote good root growth. Keep the soil evenly moist throughout this period.

YOU CAN START FORCING the bulbs when leaves begin to push upward—usually sometime after January 1. Bring the pots indoors, a few each week so you will have blooms over a longer period, to a sunny, cool (55 to 70°) place and keep the soil moist at all times. The cooler the air, the longer the flowers will last. Keep bulbs away from sources of heat, such as radiators and gas heaters. Bring all pots to be forced into warmth and light by late February.

PROBLEMS IN FORCING BULBS are few, but here are some to expect. Tulips almost always show some aphids, either on the leaves when they emerge from the soil, or on the flower buds. Spray them carefully with a houseplant aerosol. Flower buds of forced bulbs will blast (fail to open) if the soil is allowed to dry out severely after they've begun to grow. Sometimes bulbs have basal rot. This is seldom your fault. If foliage suddenly turns yellow, stops growing, give it a gentle tug. Chances are you'll find it loose in the pot, and a rootless, rotted bulb in the soil. Destroy by burning.

AFTER THE FLOWERS FADE, keep the foliage in good health by providing moisture and sunlight. As soon as danger of hard freezing is past outdoors, move them to an out-of-the-way place where the foliage can continue to mature and store up strength for another year's blooms. Although the bulbs will not be up to forcing another year, you will find them useful additions for the outdoor

Store labeled potted bulbs in a cool, frost-free place as they develop their root system. Temperatures of 35° to 55° are preferable.

garden. Plant them there when you bring them from the house, or leave them in the pots until the following autumn, transferring them then to the open ground.

NARCISSUS. These daffodil relatives with fragrant flowers are not hardy outdoors in areas where severe freezing occurs. No matter where you live, however, they are delightful subjects for forcing in a semisunny to sunny location. The bulbs are available in autumn. Plant them in moist pebbles in a bowl, or pot them in

Keep sprouting bulbs cool and moist until time to bring indoors for forcing into bloom. These daffodils are ready to bring inside.

Colorful daffodils brighten an otherwise bleak winter view. Keep flowering plants as cool as possible indoors and keep soil evenly moist during blooming period.

After flowers fade, put bulbs (with foliage still on) in an out of the way place so they can continue growing to store up energy in the bulb for next season.

a mixture of equal parts soil, sand and peat moss, kept moist. Either way, place the bases of the bulbs to a depth of 1 to 1½ inches in the growing medium, then water thoroughly. Drain, and set away in a cool (50° to 65°—no warmer, if possible), dark place for the roots to form. After the bulbs have a good root system—which usually takes two to four weeks—they may be brought to warmth and bright sun. There they quickly will send up the fragrant clusters of white or gold bloom.

After forcing paper-whites or paper-yellows, if you live where winter cold dips below 20°, discard the bulbs. In the South, plant them in the garden outdoors. But don't try to force them again. Buy new stock each year.

DAFFODILS TO FORCE. 'King Alfred' and 'Golden Harvest' are classic, golden, big daffodils that force perfectly. 'President Lebrun' has pale yellow petals and a dark golden cup and forces well. Short cup varieties good for forcing: 'John Evelyn' and 'Scarlet Leader.' Miniatures, such as 'W.P. Milner,' 'March Sunshine' and *Narcissus obvallaris,* (Lent-lily) force beautifully and take up little space.

TULIPS TO FORCE. 'Brilliant Star,' 'Ibis,' 'Prince of Austria,' 'Rising Sun,' 'Murillo,' 'Scarlet Cardinal,' 'Willemsoord,' 'Scarlet Admiral,' 'Bartigon,' 'Niphetos,' 'Rose Copland,' 'William Pitt,' 'Gudoshnik,' 'Golden Harvest' and 'Fantasy.'

HYACINTHS TO FORCE include 'Jan Bos,' 'L'Innocence,' 'Bismarck,' 'Gertrude,' 'Lady Derby,' 'La Victoire,' 'Grand Maitre,' 'Ostara,' 'Perle Brilliante,' 'City of Haarlem,' 'Queen of Pinks' and 'King of Blues.'

"LITTLE" BULBS such as crocuses, snowdrops and grape-hyacinths *(Muscari)* sometimes are forced, but they are so fleeting indoors that it is really a shame to waste time on them. They last days or even weeks longer when planted naturally outdoors.

OTHER BULBS TO FORCE in addition to the standbys include calla-lily *(Zantedeschia),* the amaryllis *(Hippeastrum),* Cape lily *(Veltheimia viridifolia),* freesia, iris *(I. reticulata* and *I. tingitana),* the Easter lily *(Lilium longiflorum),* shamrock *(Oxalis)* and Squills *(Scillea sibirica).* Some of these are discussed in our section on dormancy beginning on page 63.

FORCING HYACINTHS IN WATER. The hyacinth bulb can be grown in water placed in specially designed containers or jars or can be put in any type vase that will hold the bulb in the top and allow the roots to reach into the bottom section. Fill vase so base of the bulb just "kisses" the water. Change water every three or four weeks. A small piece of charcoal in the water will keep the water sweet and retard harmful bacteria from developing. Place in a dark, cool area until the roots are developed before moving to light. Change water weekly. Flowers and foliage develop rapidly. Use any of the varieties listed on this page.

Forcing flowering branches

The delicate beauty of long willowy branches of apple, cherry, forsythia, pussy willow and flowering quince can bring springtime beauty indoors in the midst of winter. Two- to three-foot branches should be cut during the first two or three months of the year.

Be careful when cutting not to ruin the shape of the tree or shrub. Smash the cut ends of the branches with a hammer to help the branches absorb more water. Place them in a large container of water in a moderately cool (60-70°), bright room. Change water every few days. In about two weeks the fragile blossoms will appear. Do not cut branches until tiny buds are formed. If cut too soon flowers will not open.

Forcing annual flowers indoors

Some of summer's brightest annual flowers force easily indoors in a location which receives full sun and a moderately cool, moist atmosphere. (Browallia and torenia will do with less sun—good east sunlight is ample.) Pots of summer flowers or cut blooms from your window garden will make delightful additions to your mid-winter table setting. In addition to making your own indoor garden colorful, they will make cheerful gifts for friends.

A temperature range of 60 to 70° is ideal for forced annuals. Pot them in a mixture of equal parts soil, sand and peat moss, and keep evenly moist.

Fertilize biweekly with liquid house-plant food. Pinch growing tips as necessary to encourage compact plants. Aphids are likely to be troublesome. For control tips, see page 17.

Discover the pleasures of spring branches, perennials and even annuals forced during the winter season. Here are a few to try. (clockwise, beginning top right) Sweet violet, crabapple, morning glory, ageratum, lily-of-the-valley, crabapple and nasturtium. Although these present a little more difficulty than the hardy bulbs, their lovely flowers make the efforts seem worthwhile.

To grow ageratum, sweet alyssum, dwarf balsam, borwallia and dwarf cockscomb indoors for winter and early spring bloom, sow seeds in early August. The same goes for dwarf marigolds, sweet peas, nasturtiums and morning-glories. Transplant to individual pots as soon as seedlings are large enough. As they fill one pot with roots, transfer them to a larger size, stopping with 5- to 7-inch containers. Provide trellis or strings for morning-glory and sweet pea vines. Try hanging baskets for the trailing plants.

To grow lobelia, flowering tobacco (nicotiana), petunia, snapdragon, torenia and verbena indoors, dig plants from the outdoor garden before frost in autumn. Disturb roots as little as possible, and plant in 5- to 10-inch containers. Cut back leaves and stems severely to encourage strong new growth. Keep plants in shade and coolness for a few days while they accustom themselves to the pots. Then place in a sunny window and keep moist.

Forcing hardy perennials

This is a specialized area of gardening that few ever try. However, if you have a perennial border that abounds with hosta, bleeding heart, astilbe or lily-of-the-valley, try your hand at forcing these some winter. Here's how you do it:

Dig vigorous clumps in early fall, trim them back, and pot in a moist mixture of soil, sand and peat moss. Then put them in a coldframe, unheated garage or cool attic, where severe freezing will not occur. In mid-January or early February, begin to bring the pots indoors to a moderately cool (60 to 70°), sunny window sill. Keep the soil evenly moist. When leaf growth becomes active, fertilize biweekly with regular house-plant food. If all goes well, you will be rewarded with some of spring's loveliest flowers weeks, even months, out of season.

After forcing hardy perennials, replant them in the garden outdoors. Do not try to force the same clumps again for at least two years.

45

King Louis will have nothing on you...

when you grow your own orangerie in pots

The idea of fruit trees in containers is by no means a new one. The most famous was the orangerie constructed at Versailles for Louis XIV. His whims included having the citrus trees uprooted, the roots dried, bathed in milk and replanted in order to force the trees to bloom. And to produce fruit out of season, he placed potted trees in heated greenhouses. On a smaller scale and with much less effort, you can enjoy the beauty Louis did by growing dwarf citrus in pots.

All of the dwarf trees described here need direct sun at least half of every bright winter day, comfortable room temperatures and moist, humusy soil (equal parts of garden loam, peat moss and sand). Feed with a liquid house-plant food every two to four weeks, and give the plants a shower with tepid water once a month. Keep outdoors during frost-free weather.

Invest only in dwarf varieties developed specifically for pot culture. These will produce fragrant flowers all year and edible fruit. If leaf yellowing occurs, correct by using a fertilizer labeled for acid-loving plants.

To produce fruit indoors, where presumably there are no bees buzzing around, you may need to do some pollinating. With an artist's brush, transfer pollen from the stamen of one flower to the stigma (the pistil end protruding beyond the petals) of another.

Calamondin (*Citrus mitis*). This dwarf citrus will produce abundant 1- to 2-inch orangelike fruits every month of the year. Leave them on the tree to brighten your surroundings, or use them to make marmalade.

Otaheite Orange (*Citrus taitensis*). A miniature version of the sweet orange, this plant produces 1- to

In summer or in warm climate regions you can grow oranges in outdoor containers. In cooler areas they work quite well in sunny windows. Not only will you enjoy the fruits and lovely foliage, but the deliciously fragrant flowers make them worth growing. Fruit is good in drinks.

2-inch fruits. These, however, have more the taste of a lime than an orange, and will remain on the tree for as long as two years.

Ponderosa Lemon (*Citrus limonia* "Ponderosa"). Probably the most spectacular of the dwarf citruses, this one has glossy green leaves, sharp spines and lemons that weigh from 1 to 3 pounds. Each one takes about six months to mature, but this plant will have fruit at varying stages of maturity year 'round. When fruits reach maturity, you will need to prop them with stakes.

Meyer or Chinese Lemon (*Citrus limonia meyeri*). This dwarf tree is a relatively old variety, bearing flowers that range in color from lavender to

white, followed by bright yellow lemons. These are excellent for cooking.

Persian Lime. For full-sized limes, this is the dwarf citrus to grow. The fruits are bright, chartreuse-green and the plant is easily kept under 2 feet.

Other dwarf citruses available are: grapefruit, limequat, tangello, citron, tangerine and Nagami kumquat.

Fruiting pot plants

Here are more ornamentals—some with edible fruit—that are easily grown in pots.

Natal-plum 'Fancy' (*Carissa macrocarpa*) is a hybrid that bears white,

Many fruiting plants can be grown in containers either indoors or out depending on your climate and lighting. Any of them can produce year round fruit in greenhouse environments. Here are some possibilities, beginning top left and reading clockwise: Ponderosa lemons, small plants with giant fruits; a red-leafed dwarf banana, enjoyable for its foliage even-without fruits; an orange tree from the gardens of King Louis at Versailles; luscious strawberries in a wooden hanging basket; tart tangerines; and even juicy peaches.

starlike flowers and red, cranberry-flavored fruit that can be used to make a fine jelly.

Pyracantha 'Red Elf' grows clusters of vivid scarlet berries in autumn and winter. Though the berries are inedible, they make this bushy plant a most attractive container grower.

Dwarf Pomegranate (*Punica granatum nana*) bears delicate red flowers on branches of pale green leaves in summer. Tiny, edible fruits appear in autumn. Another variety (*P. 'Chico'*) does not bear fruit, but has 1-inch, orange, carnationlike flowers.

Mistletoe fig covers itself with tiny red fruits. These are inedible, but quite decorative. The showy foliage can be trained and pruned to any shape.

Dwarf bananas (species of *Musa*) are a must for every plant lover. Graceful ornamentals, they have wide green leaves contrasted with brightly colored bracts and fruit. During the Victorian era in Europe, they were referred to as ''table banana'' because the entire potted plant was used to decorate banquet tables.

Pineapple guava (*Feijoa sellowiana*) bears spectacular 1- to 2-inch red flowers and green, edible fruit on a small evergreen tree or shrub. Root it from cuttings during warm weather (needs high humidity) in sand or perlite. Then grow in loamy soil with plenty of sand and humus.

Arabian coffeetree has large, shiny leaves, fragrant white flowers and bright red berries.

South American tree tomato (*Cyphomandra betacea*) grows delicious, egg-shaped, red fruits that are sweeter than ordinary tomatoes, and excellent for making jams.

Other fruiting plants that will thrive in containers are: Dwarf pineapple, Surinam cherry (eugenia), the tea of commerce (*Thea sinensis*), cherry tomatoes, such as 'Tiny Tim,' pepper (*Piper magnificum*), Christmas pepper (*Capsicum annuum*) and the runnerless strawberries, such as 'Catherine,' 'Baron Solemacher' and the variegated form, *Fragaria vesco albo-marginata*.

Figs– one to eat, many to enjoy

Grow fruiting trees regardless of where you live; also lofty, leafy trees and miniature creepers

This large diverse family of tropical trees includes not only the edible fig, but a number of ornamentals perfect for container gardening.

The weeping fig, *F. benjamina,* has come to a prominent position in the container plant world and is used by a great many designers. It is easy to see why this tree is selected for a special place in a well-appointed space. The bark is birchlike with graceful branches loaded with glossy, willowlike leaves. Unfortunately large specimens have been overused and abused by placement in the wrong environments as mere decorations until the tree is practically an endangered species. The plant is available in size from 2 to 15 feet. Give it good light and evenly moist soil, with moderately high humidity. Be prepared for a period of adaptation to its new environment. Often the tree will lose most of its leaves upon moving. Proper care will make it flourish again. *F. nitida* is a similar fig with smaller leaves growing in an upright, compact shape.

Indian rubber plants. *F. elastica* and the larger leaved *F. elastica decora* are old favorites. They have bold deep green leaves on stems from 2 to 10 feet tall. *F. elastica variegata* has colorful leaves that make a moire of grass green, metallic gray and creamy yellow.

Creeping fig. *F. pimula* has tiny heart-shaped leaves. This fast-growing trailer is a good plant for hanging baskets or a cascading shelf plant, as well as thriving in a terrarium and climbing on a damp surface. It likes moisture and shade. *F. radicans variegata* is a colorful climber or trailer for humid locations.

The fiddleleaf fig *(F. lyrata,* often called *F. pandurata)* is a striking container plant. It has durable, papery leaves of deep green with pleasing, fiddle shape. Grows to a height of five to ten feet.

Mistletoe fig is an interesting miniature upright tree, *F. diversifolia,* growing up to about 36 inches tall, with many Lilliputian-perfect figs of no food value. Its small rounded leaves are flecked with translucent silver. In bright sun the fruits turn red.

The edible fig tree is *F. carica* with varieties producing green, yellow or purplish fruit. It is among the easiest deciduous fruit trees to grow. Plant in large tubs with ordinary garden soil, give sun and keep moist during growing season. In cold climates the trees will need complete winter protection. Dwarf forms are available which make seasonal mobility easier.

Above is the old favorite Indian rubber plant, Ficus elastica, *a virtually indestructible house plant. Its bold form makes it a favorite of architects and designers. The specimen* F. benjamina, *on the left, forming a canopy over the day bed, thrived in a New York City apartment with good light. The humidity from the radiator pebble tray is good for all the plants shown here.*

Flowers everyday

House plants that almost never stop blooming, plus all-year bulbs and seasonal flowering plants.

Plants in this group will provide you with both the pleasure of something to look forward to and the enjoyment of whatever is in bloom at the moment. By selecting several species of blooming plants that come into flower either seasonally or continually, it is possible for you to have flowers in container plants every day of the year.

In the winter, flowering plants need a few hours of direct sun to bloom well, even the kinds that thrive in shade in summer. Additional humidity in the air around flowering plants will help them develop an abundance of full-size flowers.

The plants in this section have been divided into three categories: First, those that provide blooms throughout the year, regardless of season. Second, on page 60 are presented three bulb flowers that display attractive foliage all year and blooms at various times. The third group represents plants that bloom seasonally, including florists' gift plants, which must be given copious amounts of water to keep leaves and flowers full of life. Through good culture, some of these plants can be kept and

◊

Hanging baskets of blooming plants add color to outdoor summer patio in top photo. Bottom, left to right, shows primroses, columnea, oxalis and African violets for year 'round bloom.

helped to bloom again either indoors or in the outdoor garden; others are best discarded at the end of their blooming period (such as calceolaria and cineraria).

You will find other flowering container plants in this book under such sections as ''Shrubs on the Move,'' ''Whatever Happened to Winter?'' and ''Summer Flowers, Winter Sleepers.''

PHOSPHORUS PROMOTES BLOOMS. A water-soluble fertilizer with high phosphorus content (5-10-5, for example) will hurry otherwise healthy plants into bloom. Use plant food according to package directions. Some growers of African violets and begonias use this analysis or a similar one each month, feeding with a more evenly balanced fertilizer in-between times (23-21-17, for example).

African violet

Alphabetically and in popularity, these plants—originally collected in Africa in the late 19th century—come first in a listing of flowering plants. No other plant equals *Saintpaulia* in ability to thrive and bloom indoors for months on end. With a few plants and proper care it is possible to have continual blooms year-round.

Leaves are velvety, dark green broad ovals, slightly hairy, on short stalks growing in rosette fashion. Flowers may be single or double, fringed or ruffled, in white or shades of pink, red, violet, purple or blue.

Despite their reputation for being temperamental, African violets are no more difficult than many other container plants. They simply want plenty of light, but no burning sun (they

Pots of African violets are combined in a basket of fern and Chinese evergreen.

can take more in winter), evenly moist soil at all times and good humidity. African violets also thrive under artificial lights (see page 9), making a colorful garden possible even in dark hallways of your home.

Year-round African violets in many colors.

Those with plain green leaves are termed ''boy,'' and those with frilly, notched and ruffled leaves, often with a large white area in the center, are called ''girl.'' These terms have nothing whatever to do with the ability of the plants to bloom; all of them will bloom profusely when provided good growing conditions.

African violets flower best with only one crown (area where stems come together and join the roots). New crown growth can be removed and used for rooting new plants. Other means of propagation are discussed beginning on page 19.

There are thousands of named African violets from which to choose. Consult local experts or plant catalogs for varieties you find most appealing.

Remember, African violets need good filtered light, moisture (see special watering directions on page 12), regular feedings and special, pasteurized soil of equal parts loam, sand and peat moss; pre-packaged special mediums are recommended.

Begonia

This plant family represents a vast source of beauty for the container gardener. There are miniatures no bigger than a tea-cup, towering plants the size of bushes or even trees, and a full range in between.

The common wax or annual begonias *(B. semperflorens)* have fine, fibrous root systems which send up cupped, roundish leaves set on crisp, fleshy stems, with an endless number of flowers. In fact, *semperflorens* means ''everblooming.'' A basket of these is shown on page 58. Best growth and blooms come from seedlings, started in early winter each year (page 23); otherwise, take cuttings of stems with branches.

Choose from varieties with single, semidouble or fully double flowers.

Sunlight and every-other-week feedings of fertilizer keep wax begonias in bloom. Pot in a mix of equal parts soil, sand and peat—or use a soilless, pre-mixed medium. Allow this to dry slightly between waterings.

Angel-wing begonias combine beautiful foliage with clusters of bloom in pink, red, orange or white. They have cane- or bamboo-like stems, swollen at the joints. Kusler hybrids sold by begonia specialists are the best.

Some upright, branching begonias defy neat classification. They borrow and combine characteristics from *semperflorens,* angel-wing and hairy-leaved (page 68). 'Odorata Alba' and 'Tea Rose' even have lightly scented flowers.

Other miscellaneous begonias include excellent, easy-to-grow basket varieties: 'Alpha Gere,' *B. macrocarpa,* 'Limminghai,' 'Marjorie Daw' and the new Rieger hybrids.

Be sure to consider also the beefsteak and other rhizomatous begonias, discussed with foliage plants, page 68.

Some of many flowering begonias: angel-wing, Rieger hybrid and Semperflorens.

Columnea

There are some 150 different species of this member of the Gesneriad Family. They come from Central and South America and the West Indies, and their natural habitat is the damp, tropical forest. They make wonderful container plants, adapting well to indoor conditions and, since they are semiupright or trailing plants, look particularly well in hanging baskets as shown here. The brightly-colored, tubular flowers, which come in orange, scarlet and yellow will bloom all through the winter. Flowers range in size from ½ inch to 4 inches according to the variety. Leaves vary also from tiny, button size to 3 inches in length. They need semishade and moist air.

Brightly colored Columnea *flowers.*

Crossandra

This lovely flower belongs to the Acanthus Family and comes from India. Seldom growing higher than 1 foot if kept indoors in a container, it has glossy, green leaves and tubular, orange flowers that expand at the top, and bloom almost continuously. It needs a warm atmosphere and must be kept evenly moist but never sodden. Grow it in a mixture of half peat moss and half potting soil. Great for fluorescent culture.

Flame-violet

The *Episcia* is a relative of the African violet. It is grown primarily for beautiful foliage, but whenever days are sunny and the air warm and humid, it will bloom a festive show of scarlet, yellow and blue flowers. *Episcia reptans,* the flame-violet, started the popular trend of growing these tropical beauties.

Although beautiful in regular flowerpots, episcias are at their best in hanging baskets, because, like strawberries, they have "runners" or stolons which cascade gracefully from the mother plant.

Episcias resent cold; they like humidity, but will tolerate average house conditions if soil is kept evenly moist.

Cheery geraniums in spite of outside rains.

Geraniums

These South African plants appeal to almost everyone. And they are versatile! If you like to collect things, then geraniums are for you; there are thousands of species and named varieties, each slightly different from the others. Cheerful red or pink geraniums have convinced many people that they would like to try their hand at pot gardening—and for this same charm, interior decorators find geraniums irresistible, if a bit difficult to handle where sunlight isn't abundant.

Common geraniums are hybrids of *Pelargonium hortorum;* often called *zonale* because of the darker green or blackish zone in each leaf. Varieties are available in red, pink, apricot, tangerine, salmon and white.

Dwarf geraniums stay under 8 inches in height, and will grow for many months, even years, in a 2- to 4-inch pot.

Fancy-leaf geraniums belong in the same classification as common kinds. They have vari-colored leaves, often in beautiful bronzes, scarlets and creamy yellows.

Ivy-leaf geraniums, varieties of *Pelargonium peltatum,* bear leathery leaves with a shape uncannily like that of English ivy, to which they are in no way related. They excel in hanging baskets, but need full sun indoors and a moist, cool atmosphere. The flowers, often veined with a darker shade of their color, come in showy clusters, sometimes nearly smothering the plant.

There are all kinds of geranium oddities; there's a group with prickly stems, called "cactus." *Pelargonium* 'Poinsettia' may have quilled and squarish red or pink petals. *P.* 'Jeanenne' has single, salmon-color flowers pinked along the edges like a Sweet William. There are also bird's-egg, New Life, phlox and rosebud geraniums, climbing kinds and many more.

Impatiens

These are sometimes called sultanas or patience plants. The plants most commonly grown today are hybrids of *Impatiens sultanii* and *I. holstii*. Many outstanding varieties are easily grown from seeds sown in warmth and moisture in early spring. The low growing plants have small, flat flowers that literally cover the dark green, maroon or variegated green-and-white leaves. Impatiens thrives in shaded areas outdoors, but needs some sunlight and moist air in the house.

Upper photo: Variegated Impatiens *in bloom. Lower photo: Unusual flowers of lipstick vine,* Aeschynanthus.

Lipstick vine

In a sunny east window, or in similar light indoors or outdoors (in warm weather), this is a superb basket plant. *Aeschynanthus lobbianus* has waxy leaves on stems to 2 feet long. Off and on through the year clusters of buds form at the ends of these, each fuzzy red flower bud nestled in a maroon-brown calyx—hence, lipstick vine. Grows beautifully in a soilless medium. Keep nicely moist.

Miniature roses duplicate larger garden forms of hybrid tea roses. Here is a mixed bouquet of tiny varieties.

Miniature roses

These plants are perfect copies in miniature of the foliage and blooms of the outdoor hybrid tea floribunda or moss roses. They are available in an assortment of colors, and by careful pruning, are easily kept under 12 inches in overall height. Flowering will occur with moderate warmth (62 to 72°), at least 4 hours direct sunlight daily, and moist, fresh air. They will also thrive under artificial lighting (see page 9). Buy potted miniature roses from garden centers or any mail-order rose specialist.

Oxalis

These plants have cloverlike leaves that fold tightly together at dusk and open again each morning. Even those grown under fluorescent lights close up at sundown. Many kinds make outstanding pot plants and elegant hanging basket subjects. Grand Duchess *(Oxalis variabilis)* has large white, pink or rose flowers. Bermuda buttercup *(O. cernua* and its double-flowered form) has yellow, fragrant flowers. *O. rubra* (sometimes called *crassipes* or *rosea)* has pink flowers. *O. ortgiesii* is the tree oxalis that grows to 24 inches, with yellow flowers. *O. deppei* has pink flowers and is called lucky clover. These plants like sun and moisture, except during dormant periods (see pages 63-65).

Two examples of flowers from the passion flower vines. Indoors they can be grown in pots to frame a window by attaching them to cord.

Passion flower

This vine is grown for its fascinating flowers. *Passiflora pfordtii* (sometimes called *P. alato-caerulea)* grows a

beautiful flower that combines colors of creamy white, pink and blue. Red-flowered *P. coccinea* will bloom well through the winter and spring in a sunny location indoors. The rapid-growing vine likes a moist, sunny environment and must have something on which to attach its tendrils. Try a trellis or ceiling-to-floor pole, or use twine and train it to frame a window.

Shrimp plant

The curious bracts of this plant *(Beloperone guttata)* remind many people of shrimp. From these are borne small white flowers, typical of the Mint Family. After the flowers are gone, the bracts remain for weeks, and it is not unusual for this plant to be in bloom constantly. The original species has pinkish bronze bracts; 'Yellow Queen' has chartreuse. Both are good for pots and hanging baskets; put them in a sunny place and keep their soil on the dry side.

Waxy yellow bloom of Aphelandra.

Zebra plant

Aphelandra, of the Acanthus Family, is a tropical evergreen that has been recently added to the list of indoor plants now available. Aphelandra has dark leaves with striking, light-colored veins, which explains its common name. Of all the species, *A. squarrosa louisae* from Brazil is the most spectacular. It has spikes of waxy bright yellow bracts and white flowers rising above emerald green leaves, and other species have bracts that are red or orange. It is not an easy plant to keep blooming outside a greenhouse; it needs a lot of light and moist air to encourage the growth of flowers. Be sure the soil is always kept damp. Pot in standard mix but with doubled peat. After flowering, cut stems back, or lower leaves will drop, giving the plant a leggy appearance. Feed with weak liquid fertilizer every two weeks in summer.

Blue umbels of Agapanthus *bulbs.*

Agapanthus

In Southern California this plant is almost as familiar as the geranium is elsewhere. Unfortunately most gardeners in cold climates don't realize what a fine pot plant it is. Lily-of-the-Nile has evergreen, amaryllislike leaves and intermittently through the year umbels of blue or white flowers. Keep evenly moist and feed regularly. Indoors give it as much sun as possible; outdoors, sun or shade is acceptable.

Clivia

Grandmother's Kafir-lily was *Clivia miniata,* an amaryllis relative with fans of dark, evergreen leathery leaves. These provide a perfect foil for the strong, upright stems topped with umbels of salmon-pink flowers that appear in spring or summer. Several strains and varieties are available in outstanding colors and shapes. Pollinate and reap further reward—the seeds have a bright, cherry-red color and stay on for months.

Tulbaghia

This perennial from South Africa belongs to the Lily Family. *T. fragrans,* from the Transvaal, sometimes called pink agapanthus, is an especially attractive variety. It has a slender stalk that grows up to 18 inches, crowned with a cluster of small, lavender-pink, fragrant flowers. These will bloom all through the winter months. This plant does well indoors with cool temperatures and some fresh air.

Anthurium

This exotic plant from the American tropics has beautiful heart-shaped or lancelike leaves in rich shades of green or variegated with white, some with rose underneath. The flowers are in brilliant oranges and reds or soft white, greenish or pink. Most of the color is in the heart-shaped spathe surrounding the tiny flowers. All varieties love humidity and warmth.

Anthurium *is grown for lovely foliage as well as heart-shaped, long-lasting spathes.*

Bird-of-paradise

This member of the Banana Family, known botanically as *Strelitzia reginae,* is one of the most exotic and easiest to grow of all pot plants. Throughout the year it has showy fans of blue-green leaves. During warm seasons, mature plants send up stalks topped with fascinating birdlike flowers that combine colors of golden orange and peacock blue; these are borne out of green bracts edged with dark red.

Calceolaria

These plants have vividly colored pouch-shaped flowers from late winter until hot weather kills the

Pocketbook plant or Calceolaria.

plants. Few growers will go to the trouble it takes to raise them from seeds which must be planted in a cool moist place in spring or summer for blooms the following year. If you receive one as a gift, keep it cool and moist in semisun. The smaller-flowered yellow calceolaria seen in California nurseries in winter makes a splendid basket flower in frost-free winter climates, or for a cool greenhouse.

Christmas cactus

This perennial favorite is known botanically as *Schlumbergera bridgesi,* a complicated name for a very un-complicated plant. The similar Thanksgiving cactus is *Zycocactus truncatus.* It has leaves with two opposite pointed tips, compared to the smooth-edged Christmas cactus leaf ends. Cool nights and short days induce buds in the fall.

Chrysanthemums

Called "mums" for short, potted plants from the florist will last days, even weeks longer, if you keep them cool, moist and provide a little sunlight daily. If there are flower buds coming, feed bi-weekly with a plant food. When the plants begin to wither, set them aside in a cool place. Keep the soil barely moist and plant outdoors in early spring. Cut the old stems back to the ground.

Plant chrysanthemums in containers as you would in the ground. These can be left outdoors or brought in while in bloom. Chrysanthemums also make showy hanging baskets and can be trained as cascades or standards.

Cineraria

The Canary Islands gave us *Senecio cruentus,* a plant that grows small daisylike flowers in a rainbow of vivid colors blanketing the bright green leaves. Keep florist plants as cool as possible, in good light, and water freely. The buds will continue to open for weeks, if given fertilizer. Remove old flowers, making way for buds still forming. When buds stop coming, discard the plant.

Vivid flowers of the cineraria.

Delicate butterfly-like blooms of the Cyclamen *enjoy cool temperatures.*

Cyclamen

A thick leaved plant of silvery green, with translucent stems and veins, *C. persicum* produces showy butter-fly-like blossoms in white and shades of pale pink through vivid reds, some ruffled and variegated.

Cyclamen florist plants are often received as gifts. Most people prefer to discard the cyclamen after its blooming season, but you may like to try to keep yours. Place in semi-sun, away from drafts, and keep soil moist at all times, watering from below to keep foilage dry. New buds can be encouraged by applying liquid fertilizer every two or three weeks.

After the flowers cease to come, keep leaves in good growth. This will maintain the health of the tuber which will send up next year's flowers. In early summer, begin a dormancy period as described on page 63.

Easter lily

Lilies grow well in containers, and the fragrant white *Lilium longiflorum* is a favorite. Keep florist plants moist and provided with some sunlight. Cut flowers as they wither, but leave foliage to keep growing and storing energy in the bulb. Pots can be placed outdoors and will often produce a second bloom in a single season.

Huge clusters of small Hydrangea *flowers.*

Hydrangea

Potted hydrangeas are varieties of *H. macrophylla*, a Japanese plant. Those received as gift plants need abundant moisture to keep the foliage and flowers in good condition; if the soil dries, they will wilt badly. The flower buds form during one summer for the following year's blooms. Temperatures below 25° kill the buds.

Jerusalem cherry

This colorful relatives of the eggplant and potato is *Solanum pseudo-capsicum* with small leaves and white flowers, producing red or yellow round fruits. Provide coolness and lots of moisture. Cut back drastically after the fruiting season. Place out-doors during warm weather in a shady spot. Proper culture can produce a large, woody shrub.

Bright pink King's crown blossoms.

King's crown

Jacobinia carnea, shown here, is a bushy tropical plant with pink flowers and corrugated dark green leaves. It is best grown from tip cuttings started in the winter for summer bloom, in summer for winter flowers. Culture the same as geraniums, but with a little more moisture is fine. There is also a variety with tangerine flowers.

Unrivaled beauty of orchids in bloom.

Orchids

A collection of orchids will provide blooms year 'round, and there are many that will prosper in a window garden or under fluorescent lights. If you'd like to experiment with orchids, start with *Cattleya, Epidendrum, Oncidium* and *Paphiopedilum* (sometimes called Cypripedium or ladyslipper orchid). Study catalogs from orchid growers and read books on their culture. Orchid growing is challenging but rewarding.

Poinsettia

Of Mexican origin, *Euphorbia pulcher-rima* should be kept out of drafts in a warm place, and soil should be evenly moist. After the colorful bracts (we think of them as flowers) fall, set the plant in a cool room and let the soil stay nearly dry until spring. Then bring to sunny warmth, water well and watch for new growth. Repot in new soil and cut back canes to 6 inches from the pot rim. Poinsettias can be grown in a sunny interior or a protected area outdoors. Pinching out encourages more branches, and thereby, more blooms. Bring indoors in autumn when nights begin to cool. Keep in absolute darkness from sun-down to sun-up to assure holiday blooms.

Poinsettia is the most famous Euphorbia.

Summer flowers, winter sleepers... and vice versa

Like the cycle of hardy spring bulbs, these fair-weather bulbs grow, bloom and rest, but they can't withstand freezing.

All plants grow in a cycle which includes a resting period. With many foliage and flowering container plants, this is hardly noticeable, but the bulbs in this chapter require a real rest, a season of dormancy when tired, spent top growth dies to the ground and is cut off, and the underground portion is kept dry or barely moist in a cool but frost-free, dark storage place.

In the descriptions that follow, you will find specific instructions for each kind of bulb. One of the nicest rewards in growing all of these is that each bulb grows larger—or multiplies—every year.

In their native haunts, growth and dormancy are triggered by natural rainy and dry seasons. When we tame these wildlings and turn them into sophisticated hybrids, we must also take responsibility for playing the role of mother nature in nurturing the perfect cycle from sprouting to sprouting.

Most of these bulb flowers are not particularly sensitive to day length, which means you can start the growth cycle at any time you can provide suitable temperatures, light and moisture. Achimenes and tuberous begonias require the naturally long

Ruffly velvet texture and deep rich color of a hybrid gloxinia.

days of summer to bloom well. In fact, when nights grow longer in early fall, tuberous begonias actively produce seed-bearing female flowers and fewer of the showy male flowers. And, while caladiums are grown entirely for their beautiful foliage, they too begin to spend energy producing flowers—at the expense of new leaves—at the end of summer.

While anemones, ranunculus and freesias may not be sensitive to day length, they can't tolerate hot weather, especially warm nights. In cool but frost-free winter climates, they're as easily cultivated outdoors in the garden or in pots as gladiolus are nationwide. In the North they require special care—either a cool, sunny, airy, moist greenhouse or plant room, or a fluorescent-lighted garden that has cool, fresh air.

Achimenes

These African violet and gloxinia relatives grow from inch-long, catkinlike scaly rhizomes. Today's hybrids have single or double petunialike flowers in all shades of blue, purple, red, orange, pink and white, often with a contrasting color on the flower face. For color in the shade in summer, achimenes have no equal except impatiens. They're great basket plants. In early spring, plant the rhizomes 1 inch deep in a soilless mix (Jiffy Mix, for example). Keep warm and moist. Pinch out tip growth a time or two to induce branching. Give some direct sun in spring, bright shade in summer. Never let the soil dry out. In autumn, withhold water. Store rhizomes in dry vermiculite.

Achimenes are beautiful basket plants in a wide range of color.

Amaryllis

These are among the easiest, most dependable plants for blooming indoors. Their interesting growing cycle is simple to handle. Under good growing conditions, every four leaves will store up a flower bud inside the bulb. Inexpensive American hybrids come in white and various shades of red, scarlet and pink, also white marked with red or pink. Named

Amaryllis, Hippeastrum, are among the showiest of all flowers. Giant blooms come in shades of red, pink, salmon and white.

Dutch hybrids, often costly, are magnificent in size and color purity. Latest on the scene are South African hybrids which often bloom naturally between Thanksgiving and Christmas.

To promote luxuriant leaf growth, and the formation of next season's flower buds, provide several hours' sun or bright light all day and average house warmth. Keep evenly moist at all times and feed biweekly, except in autumn. Then, let soil be dry for at least two months; when leaves dry up, remove. Keep in a cool, dry, dark closet. When buds show, or after two or three months' rest, repot and start into growth. Mealybugs are a bad amaryllis pest, especially when they get down in the neck of the bulb.

Anemone

The poppylike flower *A. coronaria* is a successful greenhouse plant, can be grown in outdoor containers in California and Florida, and works in interior spaces only if it can be kept cool (55° at night) and humid. Anemones are known for their vivid hues of red, purple, pink and blue. They also grow in white and pastels. Soak the tiny corms in water overnight before planting. Keep them cool, dark and slightly moist until evidence of growth appears. Place in an airy, sunny spot indoors or a partially shaded outdoor area. Water freely and fertilize biweekly. Anemones are susceptible to aphids. Store while dormant in a cool, dry place until time for new cycle.

Colorful poppy-like flowers rise above the fern-like foliage of Anemone. *Grow these bulbs in brilliant hues or subtle pastels.*

Caladiums

These are showy foliage plants that grow from a fleshy tuber. They

A beautiful use of caladiums in a circular planter under the fern pedestal. Many colorful patterns and combinations are available in the caladium family.

are sometimes forced into growth in winter, but do best in warm summer temperatures, moist atmosphere. Standard varieties are available at local plant counters in late winter and spring; also from most mail-order nurserymen. Beautiful new hybrids are a better buy these days..

Caladiums like warmth and humidity. In addition, they thrive in dappled sun or bright, open shade in summer. Keep moist at all times. Fertilize biweekly from spring until early fall with a well-balanced plant food. In late fall, dry off caladium plants by withholding water, and store the tubers in a warm place (60°) until spring. Wet soil during dormancy may cause them to rot.

Calla-lily

The elegant white *Zantedeschia aethiopica* blooms in winter or spring. Plant tubers in late summer. *Z. elliottiana,* with yellow flowers and silver markings on the leaves, and the new pastel hybrids, are summer bloomers. Start these tubers in late winter or early spring. Callas grow best in a sunny area. During the dormant period, keep barely moist. When evidence of growth appears, water freely. After blooms stop, and leaves turn yellow, stop watering and feeding. Rest until next season.

Fragrant gladiolus

This is the common name for *Acidanthera,* an African bulb with gladiolus foliage and fragrant white flowers, blotched with maroon. Three to six flowers grow on a stalk. Plant new corms in the spring. Keep pots in a sunny location and water freely. Store away for winter in a cool dry place. Can also be cycled as freesias.

Freesia

South African in origin, these plants grow from small corms planted an inch deep. Foliage is thin, sword-shaped. Very fragrant flowers in shades of yellow, lavender, orange and white cluster at the end of slender stems. New corms should be planted in the fall for blooms in late winter or early spring. During their growing season freesias should have sunlight, cool temperatures, moist atmosphere and soil and biweekly feedings.

They are excellent subjects for greenhouse culture. After flowers stop and leaves begin to brown, cut watering to dry off. Store corms in cool, dry place until following season.

Climbing lilies, Gloriosa, *attach their tendril-like leaf tips to trellis. Flowers are brilliantly colored and exotically shaped.*

Gloriosa

Often called climbing lily because of the way in which it climbs by means of tendril-like leaf tips. Flowers have narrow petals that curve backwards. *G. rothschildiana* produces crimson and yellow flowers. *G. simplex* is a dwarf with flowers that range from yellow to orange according to the amount of sunlight received. *G. superba* climbs up to 10 feet and has yellow flowers which mature to red.

Gloriosas grow best on a trellis or wire mesh. By varying planting times, they can bloom all through the year indoors. Give good moisture and sun during growing season. Rest after season until new growth is seen. Long roots, like a big white radish require a large pot or basket.

Gloxinias

These velvety-leaved Brazilian plants are members of the Gesneriad Family. They are known botanically as *Sinningia.* In practice, growers tend to call the natural species sinningias, and the hybrids gloxinias. Some miniatures—both hybrids and species —have ½-inch leaves and inch-long flowers almost constantly.

Hybrid gloxinias are available today in many colors and countless combinations, including petals banded with contrasting color, and solid-color petals heavily spotted or misted with another color. Some are double.

Gloxinias need humidity and full sun in winter and summer shade in order to grow and bloom. Pot the

Gloxinias come in many forms, colors and textures and bloom at different times.

tubers, whenever available, about ½ inch deep. Keep evenly moist at all times. After blooming ceases and leaf growth seems to have reached a standstill, gradually withhold water until stems and leaves die down; put pot and contents in cool, dark, mouseproof place for two to four months while the tuber rests.

During this time, keep soil just barely moist so that the tuber won't shrivel. After the resting period, repot into fresh soil, move to light and warmth; provide moisture.
Feed growing gloxinias biweekly.

Haemanthus

Umbels of tightly packed flowers are sent up by this interesting South African bulb. Foliage is green, much like the amaryllis. It is very long-lasting and requires little dormancy. The plant should receive semi-sunny light and stay evenly moist except during fall and winter rest when it should stay almost dry. Bulbs should not be repotted each year after rest, merely begin the water and light cycle again. *H. albiflos* bears white flowers during June. *H. coccineus* blooms dark-red. Salmon-red flowers are borne on *H. Katherinae* and *H. multiflorus* produces dark crimson flowers. All of the red-flowered species are commonly called blood-lilies.

Ixia

South America gives us another exotic blooming bulb called corn-lily. Tall, wiry, yet strong stems produce six or more bell-shaped flowers on a dense spike in red, violet, pink, yellow, or white, with dark centers.

Foliage is grasslike. Ixia needs full sun, lots of water during growing season; see also *Freesia* for cycle and culture.

Montbretia

This member of the Iris Family is known botanically as *Crocosmia x crocosmaeflora*. It produces a dense cluster of sword-shaped leaves. Tall flower spikes, usually branching, bear orange-red starlike blooms. Plant pots of corms in a sunny location, treat like fragrant gladiolus. Store corms in peat for winter.

Oxalis

Some species of this family grow from tubers or rhizomes such as *O. braziliensis,* sold as shamrocks by florists. Rosy-colored flowers appear above bright green leaves. Many colors and variegations of leaves and flowers are available. Oxalis can bloom at different times according to species. Keep moist during growth. Place into dormancy after leaves fade. See also page 59.

Ranunculus

These most beautiful of all buttercups produce an array of double flowers in pink, yellow, orange, red and white. Indoors or outdoors they cannot tolerate dry heat. They also require a frost-free environment. For winter bloom in a home greenhouse or plant room (should be sunny, cool, moist, airy), plant tubers in autumn, which is also the planting time for winter-spring bloom outdoors in mild climates. Aphids find young ranunculus leaves irresistible; spray to control or flowering will be impaired. While in active growth, feed every other week. When flowering stops, dry off, discard tops, remove tubers from the soil and store in dry peat or vermiculite in a frost-free place.

Outdoor pots of blooming Ranunculus.

Tuberous begonias

These showy plants have become mockingbirds of the plant kingdom. They come in carnation-, rose-, daffodil-, and camellia-flowered forms. All are spectacular plants for decorating a semi-shady terrace, patio or garden in the summer and early fall. They like a moist, humusy soil, warm days, cool moist nights and protection from hot, dry winds. For equal flower beauty Indoors in winter, grow the Rieger hybrid begonias.

Plant sprouted tubers ½ inch deep in moist, coarse leaf mold, fir bark, or peat moss and sand. Keep this evenly moist at all times, but never soggy wet. Keep in warmth (70 to 75°). Tubers are usually ready for planting February-April. After they form a good root system, pot them in a mixture of equal parts soil, sand peat moss and leaf mold; keep this evenly moist at all times. Fertilizer applied biweekly through the growing season until early fall will encourage steady, vigorous growth. Before frost is expected, bring the plants inside to a warm, dry place. Withhold water until tops die; discard the old leaves and stems, but leave the tubers in the soil. Apply a limited amount of water through the dormant period, to keep the soil barely damp.

Among the showiest flowering plants are the tuberous begonias in a great variety of forms.

Ferns, philodendrons, palms and other foliage plants

Select colorful desert or rain forest foliages, but remember green is also a color in many shades, textures and forms.

Unlike most flowering plants—which are at peak beauty for only short periods—foliage plants are handsome the year-round. You'll find unlimited variety in sizes, shapes, leaf patterns and colors.

Nature provides a mind-boggling

spectrum of colors in limitless combinations. The range of textures available in both green, variegated and unusual colors is reminiscent of department store fabric counters or grandmother's patchwork quilt.

A collection of container plants can be a veritable rainforest of humidity-loving tropicals or an arid desert of sun-worshipping cacti and other succulents. Perhaps the most pleasing garden is a blending of all types of plants from many habitats, showing great contrasts of bold forms overshadowing tiny creeping vines.

Select plants that you like, that require growing conditions suitable to your environment and that you will be happy caring for.

Most of the plants identified on the next 16 pages are durable, easily-cultivated kinds that can stand a wide range in temperatures, moisture and lighting conditions. Check our mini-encyclopedia beginning on page 90 for basic, specific information regarding culture and propagation.

Failure with foliage plants comes most often from careless watering practices—either too much or too little. Remember, with the exception of a few cacti, no plant can exist in dry, bricklike soil. Likewise, a constant saturation pleases only a few plants. See watering directions, along with other basics of container gardening beginning on page 7.

Select top quality plants from reliable sources where you can be reasonably sure they are free from disease. Consider the joy of starting new plants from seed, cuttings, air-layering or divisions.

⬆
Some of the easiest to grow house plants include these, mostly shade tolerant, species. All thrive in the temperature of the average house. Most like humidity. **A.** Dieffenbachia amoena, **B.** Dieffenbachia picta 'Superba,' **C.** Columnea 'Stavanger,' **D.** Dracaena deremensis, **E.** Guzmania berteroniana 'rubra,' **F.** Cycas revoluta, **G.** Anthurium crystallinum, **H.** Philodendron laciniatum, **I.** Chamaedorea elegans, **J.** Ficus lyatra *or* F. pandurata, **K.** Pilea cadierei, **L.** Hedera helix, **M.** Hedera helix, **N.** Monstera deliciosa *(Philodendron pertusum)*, and **O.** Asparagus densiflorus 'Sprengeri.'

Acorus

If you want a bit of white and green variegated grass to complete a planting arrangement, consider *Acorus gramineus*. It forms a grassy spray about 10 inches tall. *A. gramineus pusillus* is a miniature form with leaf fans 3 inches tall; *A calamus variegatus* is the sweet flag. It too, has beautifully variegated foliage, flat and similar to an iris. All of these like to have a soil that is constantly wet.

Hanging Asparagus densiflorus 'Sprengeri.'

Asparagus-fern

Vegetable asparagus has many tender relatives that make good container plants. African in origin, these members of the Lily Family are reliable growers, to be enjoyed in indoor or outdoor shady gardens. The feathery cool green branchlets grow on stalks that reach lengths of 1 to 6 feet, and are handsome trained on string or wire, or in hanging baskets.

A. setaceus (known until recently as *plumosus*) is the lacy "fern" often used by florists with roses. Its semi-climbing stems have prickles, and may form purple berries. Preferring an outdoor environment, it does not do well as a house plant. *A sprengeri* has coarser leaves than those of the vegetable. It is a durable plant that can live through drought, but loves humidity. Its branchlets are set with ½-inch needle-like leaves and some thorns. Fragrant, tiny white summer flowers are followed by cherry-red berries around Christmas. *A. asparagoides myrtifolius,* with broad rather than needle-like leaves, is another species cultivated by indoor gardeners. Florists call it "baby smilax," and use it in arrangements. *A. densiflorus 'Meyers'* is a relatively new addition to container plants. It forms bottle-brush-shaped spears that reach 18 inches in height. *A. densiflorus 'Myriocladus'* grows shrub-like to as high as 6 feet, with linear leaves, greenish-white flowers and reddish berries.

Aspidistra elatior 'Variegata.'

Aspidistra

This grows all over in Southern gardens, usually as a completely carefree—and therefore neglected—ground cover in dense, dark shade. Ironically, like many "folk" plants, it is not always available in nurseries. This is partly because it grows so slowly, and partly because it is not properly appreciated. As a bushy foliage pot plant, 12 to 24 inches tall and as wide, the aspidistra simply has no equal when it comes to tolerance of dim light and neglect. Wet or dry, sun or darkest shade, here's a real toughie to build your confidence as a pot plant grower indoors or outdoors. *A. elatior* has cornlike, shiny, dark green leaves to 24 inches and occasionally produces purple-brown small flowers near the base of the plant. Its variegated form is shown above. The white markings help to "light up" a dark corner, the same as sun filtering through a shade tree. A dwarf form, known as *minor,* has white-spotted black-green leaves. Try to acquire all three, then display in attractive pottery containers.

Begonia

This huge and varied family is divided into three categories: tuberous-rooted, fibrous-rooted and ornamental-leaf begonias (usually rhizomatous). The tuberous-rooted and most of the fibrous-rooted are grown for their flowers and are discussed in preceeding chapters. The plants here are treasured for their leaves.

Hairy leaf begonias have fuzzy textured leaves, some splashed with red or silver on various green backgrounds. Try growing *alleryi,* 'Mrs. Fred D. Scripps' or *drostii.* *Beefsteak or star* begonias range from miniatures to giants, with colors of silver to brown. Some are thickly succulent, often ruffled, or have smooth star-like leaves. Favorites include 'Cleopatra,' 'Texas Star,' 'Silver Star' and 'Maphil.' *Rex begonias* come in a variety of rich textures, patterns and colors. While the foliage plant coleus is often likened to a Persian carpet, rex begonias are more like a fine Aubusson. 'Merry Christmas' is the most popular named variety, but there are hundreds of others. It's fun to collect as many different ones as you can find. The stems are densely covered with glistening hairs. Some are tea-cup size, others like a bushel. The rexes thrive in warmth, high humidity and bright light, but little direct sun. They're also excellent in fluorescent-light gardens.

An easy-to-grow rhizomatous begonia which looks like a rex, but isn't is *B. masoniana* or Iron Cross. Its green leaves are marked with a cross.

Three hairy leaf begonias are among the most spectacular foliage plants. Upper right is Begonia masoniana *(Iron Cross). Others are hybrid* B. rex.

Two level, skylighted foyer of a city townhouse boasts two large specimen trees—a mature Dizygotheca elegantissima *in left foreground and* Brassaia actinophylla *(Schefflera), upper right. Ferns, other foliage plants and blooming species are used throughout the space.*

Brassaia (*Schefflera*)

Mistakenly classified as Schefflera until very recently, this beautiful evergreen tropical foliage plant is sometimes referred to as the Australian umbrella tree.

B. digitata and *B. actinophylla*—two popular species—make graceful, durable plants for pots and planters, ranging in size from 5-inch seedlings to trees 6 feet or more tall. Six to eight shiny green, pointed oval leaves grow at the end of long branches. Clusters of small flowers may be produced.

Brassaia is a good plant for well-lighted, non-sunny areas, either indoors or on the patio in summer.

Its hardiness and large scale make it a perennial favorite with designers and decorators for commercial spaces and dwellings as shown in the two-level foyer in the photograph above.

Chlorophytum comosum picturatum.

Chlorophytum

For its fountains of new plantlets which create an airy, graceful appearance, this plant gets its first common name, "spider plant." Another popular name, "airplane plant," comes from the fact that these same plantlets are born in the air, while in other plant families, the babies come by the orthodox routine of sprouting from the soil, or from seeds. The common spider plant is *Chlorophytum elatum vittatum.* Other good kinds include *C. comosum picturatum* with large, creamy bands down leaf centers and *C. comosum mandaianum* with green leaves, edged creamy white.

69

Three species of Aglaonema, *Chinese evergreen.*

Chinese evergreen

This is the popular name for *Aglaonema modestum,* a durable foliage that will grow for long periods of time in plain water. In plant stores you'll find other aglaonemas with silver-and-green leaves. These prefer soil culture. All grow amazingly well in dimly lit places. Long-lasting red berries.

Cissus capensis (above) and C. antarctica.

Cissus

These members of the Grape Family are ideal for containers; their vines will spill out of hanging baskets or cascade beautifully from pots on pedestals or shelves. Or if you like, allow the tendrils to attach themselves to string, trellis or wall. These plants withstand neglect and poor conditions, making them good office or city inhabitants. Over-watering and moving around may cause leaf fall.

C. antarctica, known as kangaroo vine because it grows by leaps and bounds, has elongated, shiny green leaves. *C. capensis* has leaves shaped similar to the oak. *C. rhombifolia* is the popular grape-ivy, with dark green leaves formed of three leaflets. *C. discolor,* the group's showy member, has rosy stems and green leaves flushed silver-rose.

Coleus

So richly colored are the leaves of this member of the Mint Family (square stems are the clue), some people simply call it "foliage." Keep growth tips pinched to promote compact branching. It's easy, fun to grow as a bush, basket or little tree. Spikes of pale blue flowers should be pinched back.

Richly colored foliage of Coleus.

Cyperus

These graceful plants look like something that ought to be growing by the Nile River. And they do love moisture; keep the pots in saucers of water. *C. papyrus,* Egyptian paper plant, has umbrellas of grassy leaves that burst out of 3-foot triangular stems. *C. alternifolius* is smaller, *C. elegans* more delicate. Unique appearance, indoors or out.

Blackish leaves of Dizygotheca elegantissima.

Dizygotheca

False aralia is another name for *D. elegantissima.* Leathery black-green leaves with lighter veins are spread fingerlike into nine segments with saw-toothed edges. You can buy thumb-pot seedlings for terrariums, or an old one big enough to sit under. *D. veitchii* is similar with coppery green leaves, reddish undersides and red veins.

Just a few of many Dracaena *species.*

Dracaena

These leafy members of the Lily Family are fascinating to collect, and then to arrange in a display as we did (photo above). Plain green *D. fragrans* occasionally yields sprays of white, fragrant flowers. It adapts well to dim light indoors. *D. deremensis* forms like 'Roehrs Gold' and 'Janet Craig' have striped leaves—truly dramatic container plants, indoors and out. *D. fragrans* varieties *massangeana* and 'Victoriae' have broader, equally showy leaves. *D. sanderiana* has white-margined green leaves on slender cane stems. *D. marginata,* little known until recently, is now one of the most common house trees. Its red-edged thin leaves grow tuft-fashion atop trunks that naturally zigzag and curve. Broad-leaved *D. godseffiana,* with white and gold splotches, is miniature by comparison to the others; may form red berries. Three look-alike, grow-alike relatives are Hawaiian ti (*Coroyline terminalis,* shown below). *Dianella* and *Pleomele.*

Coroyline terminalis, *known as Hawaiian ti.*

Dieffenbachia picta 'Rudolph Roehrs.'

Dieffenbachia

Touched to the tongue, the sap from the canelike stems of this plant can cause temporary speechlessness, hence "dumb cane" and such remarks as "mother-in-law plant" (which is actually *Sansevieria*). For planter and large container decorations, dieffenbachias have few equals as accent plants—indoors all year, or outdoors in warm weather. They are shrubby with thick stems and large, wide oblong leaves. Dieffenbachias combine many marbled shades of green, chartreuse, cream and white, with bold shape and habit. Mature plants reach ceiling height and will need air-layering to eliminate ugly, gawky stems (see page 19). Kinds like 'Rudolph Roehrs' (shown here), *D. amoena* and *D. picta* adapt well to indoor living spaces. They contrast pleasingly with cornlike dracaenas, spathiphyllums and ferns.

Fatsia

Sometimes called "aralia," *Fatsia japonica* is a handsome evergreen foliage plant with bold, palmately-lobed leaves of shiny green, occasionally white variegated. Common all-year outdoor plant in frost-free climates; should be used more indoors up North. Smaller scale *Fatshedera* is the child of fatsia and English ivy, with fatsia leaves and the growth habit of ivy.

Ferns

This group of plants is one of the oldest known to man, many varieties having been found as fossils dating from prehistoric times. Through the ages, ferns have remained among man's favored plants. Today, many varieties are available for growing as container plants either indoors or in shaded areas outdoors. Ferns make great hanging baskets, and there are tiny forms for terrariums and dish gardens.

The Boston fern *(Nephrolepis exaltata bostoniensis)* is probably the most common and easiest to grow, but there are other varieties of it, such as the frivolous 'Fluffy Ruffles,' that provide a change from the ordinary.

Holly ferns (species of *Cyrtomium*) have leathery, hollylike leaves. Various kinds of *Polypodium* especially *aureum* and its varieties) and *Polystichum* are dramatic plants with magnificent fronds.

The *Davallia* is known as "rabbit's-foot" because of its fuzzy, creeping rhizomes. Delicate, airy fronds grow from these, and this fern makes an especially beautiful hanging plant.

Staghorn ferns *(Platycerium)* resemble antlers and are best displayed in a container hung on a wall, while tiny ferns, such as *Pteris*,

Left: Large leaves of Fatsia japonica *(above) and the climbing form* Fatshedera, *a cross of fatsia and English ivy. Below: Growing in hollowed lava rock are ferns* Polystichum tsus-simense *and* Pteris cretica, *overshadowing spreading clubmoss* Selaginella kraussiana. *All these plants enjoy frequent misting with water to build up humidity.*

This plant collection includes a number of fern species. (Clockwise, beginning top left) Cibotium, *the Hawaiian tree fern growing in a bark planter; a wall of staghorns,* Platycerium, *hang like prized antlers; heavily marked* Fittonia, *(see text below); a hanging basket of* Davallia, *"rabbit's foot" fern; the furry rhizomes sprout new fronds of* Davallia; *and the delicate looking, moisture-loving maidenhair fern,* Adiantum.

make excellent accents in miniature dish garden landscapes.

The bird's-nest fern *(Asplenium nidus)* has vivid green, wide, leaflike fronds, giving it a distinctive look when displayed with other ferns.

Delicate maidenhair ferns *(Adiantum)* have many small wedge-shaped leaflets on thin wiry black stems. They require a lot of moisture.

The Hawaiian tree fern *(Cibotium)* grows long lacy fronds from a thick trunk to a height of 30 feet or more.

Fittonia

The beautiful white-veined leaves shown in the bottom right photograph of the fern collection above belong to *Fittonia verschaffeltii argyroneura.* Another variety features pink veins, while variety *pearcei* has intense red veins against olive-green papery, thin backgrounds. The plants grow semi-upright or trail gracefully over their containers. Small plants are good for terrariums.

Gynura

A sun-worshiping plant covered with brilliant purple hairs, *G. aurantiaca* (commonly called "purple passion") is especially suited to hanging baskets.

The plant should not be over pampered for its own survival. Occasionally it blooms tiny yellow flowers.

Helxine

Baby's-tears is the common name of this tiny compact creeper. The plant grows thick and dense and makes an excellent terrarium ground cover. It is a lover of humidity and grows rapidly in moist greenhouses. Both gold and green varieties are shown encircling the red iresine in the photograph here.

A Tiffany silver bowl features Iresine *encircled by two varieties of* Helxine·

Homalomena

This showy foliage plant is related to the philodendron, and shares its love for tropical warmth and moisture. *H. humilis* forms a rosette of plain-

green pointed leaves; *H. wallisii* has dark olive-green reflexed, oval leaves excitingly marked with areas of silver.

Hypoestes

This is a rapid growing plant generously freckled with pink splotches on green, oval leaves (pink polka-dot). The more sunlight it receives the more intense its markings, making a cheerful addition to your collection. Spikes of lavender flowers may appear.

Iresine

Foliage of this blood-leaf plant is intensely colored as evidenced by the red in the photograph combined with *Helxine.* Other varieties have yellow and green areas. Leaves are notched at the tips, giving the name chicken gizzard. The small plants add brilliant accents to groupings.

Ivy

Many plants are called ivy, but the most famous is *Hedera helix,* or English ivy. It is available in countless varieties. Some have typical English ivy leaves, except smaller. 'Merion Beauty' is an example. There are tiny varieties such as 'Itsy Bitsy.' Others have the same leaves, except they've been curled, waved and crinkled. 'Curlilocks' is an example. And some others have color variegations, like the yellow-gold and green 'California Gold.' All are good climbers and will attach themselves by aerial roots to rough surfaces, such as a brick fireplace wall. And they are unsurpassed ground covers for large planters. Even in poor light, a healthy plant of English ivy will decorate a coffee table for months.

Algerian ivy *(Hedera canariensis)* is also a superb foliage plant, with large bright green leathery leaves.

Ivies make excellent hanging baskets and can be trained into interesting topiary shapes for whimsical touches in plant collections. They are beautifully trained espalier-style on a trellis in containers. Trailing plants give a soft effect to groupings of container plants.

English ivy, Hedera helix 'Curlilocks' *(top photo) and Algerian ivy,* Hedera canariensis 'Variegata.' *Ivys are useful as hanging baskets, trellis and trailing plants.*

Joseph's-coat

This is the common name for *Alternanthera versicolor,* a low foliage plant with small, round corrugated leaves of red, yellow, cream, chartreuse and green. It is best used alone in a container, not combined with other plants. Pinching growing tips helps Joseph's-coat grow low and bushy *A. bettzickiana* is a miniature version.

Liriope

Part of the fun of container gardening is making attractive arrangements of your plants. For an effective accent touch of graceful, grassy leaves, grow pots of the clump-forming *Liriope muscari* (plain green leaves, violet flowers in season) and *L. m. variegata* (cream-striped leaves). The related *Ophiopogon* is equally easy to grow, also showy.

Norfolk island pine

This evergreen tree with tiers of needle-set branches is *Araucaria excelsa.* In time it grows large enough to decorate at Christmas. Needs winter warmth, but likes a summer vacation outdoors in a shady, moist spot. Seedlings are fine for dish gardens. Other araucarias, including the monkey puzzle, are less suited to container gardening.

Palms

These slow-growing plants have the ability to withstand lack of light, drafts of cold, hot or dry air and general neglect—always giving accent, mood and interest.

Miniature palm seedlings or Neanthe bella *(Chamaedorea elegans bella)* are useful in terrariums.

The "fish-tail" palms are *Caryota plumosa, C. mitis,* and *C. urens. Chamaedorea erumpens* and *C. seifritzii* are the "bamboo palms." *C. elegans* is the popular "parlor palm."

The "butterfly" palm is *Chrysolidocarpus.* An old standby is the longlasting "kentia" palm *(Howea).* Fan shaped palms are the bushy *Chamaerops, Licuala, Livistona* and *Rhapis* with bamboo-like hairy canes. A graceful fernlike palm is *Phoenix roebelenii,* the dwarf date palm.

In the right column are some popular palms. A turtle contains Chamaedorea elegans *or* Neanthe bella; Cycas *is not a palm, but a member of an ancient plant family; the "kentia" palm* (Howea) *in a glazed pot; and a small* Rhapis *grows in a desktop glazed container.*

Pandanus is an almost foolproof house plant. Corkscrew growth inspires common name, screw pine.

Pandanus

Called screw-pine because the cornlike, prickly-edged leaves spiral upward corkscrew-fashion in a compact rosette. Some are white-striped vertically, others have burgundy edges. Aerial roots grow downward, searching for moist soil. A tough, but graceful plant. Looks great in an urn, or displayed on a pedestal. Almost foolproof; pest-free.

Pellionia

Delightful foliage "fabrics" to carpet bare ground around big container plants. Or use them in terrariums, bottle gardens and baskets. *P. daveauana* has dark, brown-green leaves with a broad center area of metallic silver-green. *P. pulchra* has dark brown-green leaves heavily netted with silver-green veining. 'Argentea' is pale green and rosy.

Three peperomias include, top to bottom, P. griseo-argentea, P. griseo, and P. obtusifolia. Strange green flowers give these plants an outer space look.

Peperomia

These small plants grow mostly in compact rosettes with crinkled or plain heart-shape leaves. Spikes of tiny flowers in season make the plants look like outerspace visitors. Most common is *P. sandersi,* the watermelon-begonia. It is neither, but a member of the Black Pepper Family. There are dozens of others in cultivation, easy to grow, fun to collect. The leaves vary from black-green to glistening silver.

Philodendron

The popularity of this plant is amazing. Since the early 1940's it has come from near obscurity to become one of the most popular plants for containers. Beginning gardeners almost always have a philodendron in their collection.

Ironically, two plants most generally known as philodendrons are related, but known botanically by other names. One, also called ivy and pothos, is *Scindapsus* (See "Pothos," page 75); the other is *Monstera deliciosa,* known as *Philodendron pertusum* while it is a young plant.

Philodendron species divide themselves fairly neatly into two groups —those that climb, and those that don't (called self-heading). Hybrid-

Hybrid self-heading Philodendron 'Orlando' is one of this varied family which is always included among house plant indestructibles.

izers are crossing the two groups, however, and now there are intermediates. The climbers and semi-climbers need a moist totem pole to climb—they'll do poorly without this means of support. Materials for this support include pressed osmunda fiber (available at plant counters), and pieces of bark. Or you can make your own by wrapping a piece of ½-inch chicken-wire around moist, unmilled sphagnum moss. The air roots of the philodendron will attach themselves to the totem.

Good small, climbing or trailing philodendrons include: *P. oxycardium* (often sold as P. cordatum), *P. discolor, P. micans* and *P. sodiroi* (this one is nice for bottle gardens).

Representatives of the two groups of philodendron species—a climber, P. mamei, on the left, and a self-header, P. Weber's 'Selfheading.'

Bromeliads

Succulent Pineapple Relatives for Foliage and Flowers

Columbus discovered pineapples growing on the West Indian island of Guadeloupe on his second voyage to the New World in 1493, but it was not until around 1950 when we began to appreciate the entire Pineapple Family, the bromeliads. Showy, colorful, even bizarre, they share the edible pineapple's habit of growing a rosette of stiff leathery leaves.

In frost-free climates, these can be grown outdoors year-round, in pots, or hanging from and perching in trees. For remarkably beautiful foliage, flowers and long-lasting bracts and berries, they have no equal among other house plants. Indoors, they grow in sun or shade, do well in fluorescent-lighted gardens, and look marvelous in wall-mounted containers. There are fist-size miniatures and arm-span giants.

Most bromeliads are formed of a rosette of leaves with a cuplike empty area (the "vase") in their center. It is important that the vase be always filled with water. It's good to empty the rosette of water each time before adding more.

The plants should be grown in a coarse, open growing medium, because most bromeliads are air plants in their native haunts. Pot in a mixture of equal parts peat moss and sand; or in unshredded sphagnum moss; or in osmunda fiber. Whichever medium you choose, keep it on the dry side; pay more attention to keeping the rosettes of leaves filled with water.

Aechmea

The living vase plant, has outstanding foliage all year, plus showy spikes of pink bracts with blue flowers in season which are followed by long-

◁

Bromeliads (reading clockwise, beginning top left). Aechmea recurvata, Tillandsia, Guzmania *hanging basket, bloom of* Aechmea fasciata, Aechmea fasciata purpurea, Ananas comosus variegata, Tillandsia *on bark,* Neoregelia carolinae *and* Guzmania lingulata.

lasting scarlet berries. The common name refers to the leaf rosettes which have a long, slender tube from which the flower stem grows. In bloom, the plant appears to have provided its own vase, for the tube of leaves will hold water.

Ananas

The commercial pineapple. It grows with narrow sharp-edged gray-green leaves. Sprout your own plant by placing the cut top portion from the fruit in shallow water. There is a dwarf variety on the market, also one with variegated leaves. Fruits are grown in middle of the leaf rosette.

Billbergia

Particularly *B. nutans* (called queen's tears) is widely grown, and easy to obtain. Its rosettes are similar to a young pineapple top, except they are longer and more slender. The pendent, graceful flowers have violet-edged, green petals.

Cryptanthus

Stays within a few inches above the ground. In fact, their rosettes of leaves stay on such a horizontal plane that as a group they are called "earth stars." Small ones are good terrarium specimens.

Guzmania

Forms long yellowish leaves striped with dark red. They produce many red, white or yellow flowers in winter. Try *G. berteroniana* and *G. zahnii.*

Neoregelia

Bromeliads produce their flowers just above the water in the vase. Leaves are green with stripes of yellow, white, and rose. The area around the vase is rosy red and nestles the tiny blue flowers.

Tillandsia

Grows as a dark-green rosette of narrow long leaves. *T. lindenii* produces an ornamental spike of bright pink bracts on which splendid blue flowers bloom.

Vriesea

Has wide leaves in rosette form. *V. splendens* is zebra-striped in brown and produces a tall flame-like bract of orange. A small variety is *V. carinata* with brilliant yellow, red and green bracts and tiny short-lived yellow flowers.

Bromeliads can be propagated by division of offsets from the parents. Slice through soil with a sharp knife, taking some of the basal growth and roots. Pot the division in its own container and provide the same growing conditions as the parent plant.

Remember to keep water in the vase or cup formed by bromeliad leaves. Water must be in the vase at all times, and should be changed weekly. Roots of bromeliads should be watered sparingly, but never neglect the vase water. It is not advisable to add fresh cut flowers to the vase of the bromelied as many people do. This injures new growth and robs the plant of needed moisture.

Cacti and other succulents

This is a vast grouping of plants, all of them with the habit of storing moisture inside their fleshy stems and leaves. They come from both desert and rainforest, and not all are thorny and leafless. Lemon-vine or *Pereskia*, for example, has citruslike leaves *and* wicked thorns, plus showy, fragrant flowers and it climbs! The *Opuntia* cacti bear edible prickly-pears. If you have the collector spirit, there are enough cacti and other succulents to keep you fascinated for a lifetime.

Growing cactus

As container plants, virtually all of them have the ability to exist, if not thrive, in the normally dry, warm atmosphere of the average house.

SOME DO NEED PARTIAL SHADE, certainly protection from full, burning sun outdoors during hot weather. Generally speaking, all of them appreciate a little dryness between watering, but remember, a pot or other container of soil can become deathly dry even to these water-storing plants. A general rule is to water thoroughly, allow soil to become dry and remain dry for a couple of days before rewatering.

Mistletoe cactus

These succulents, known as *Rhipsalis*, are strange in appearance, quite like true mistletoe. They're useful in baskets, pots and planters. Most are grown for the bright green foliage, but in season the blooms are an added treat. They thrive in a moist atmosphere with some shade, very much like the Bromeliads. *Hatiora* (drunkard's dream) is related, also fun to grow.

Orchid cacti

These beautiful flowers are as lovely as orchids, but shaped more like water-lilies. Foliage is not cactuslike, but leafy, and some make great basket plants in a semishady spot. *Epiphyllum* is the Latin name and the most common species, *E. oxypetalum,*

*Shade tolerant succulents: **A.** Hoya bella, **B.** Pedilanthus tithymaloides, **C.** Senecio rowelayanus, **D.** Euphorbia tirucalli, **E.** Hylocereus, **F.** Scilla violacea, **G.** Hoya carnosa, **H.** Rhipsalis capilliformis and **I.** Synadenium grantii rubra.*

is one of the easiest of the so-called night-blooming cereus. Specialists who sell by mail and locally can recommend small-growing hybrids, best suited to growing indoors up North in freezing weather.

Other cacti

Serious collectors spend years searching out odd and unusual cacti. They've been so successful, in fact, that it is a bewildering decision to choose only a few plants. The best way is to visit specialists (or study their catalogs), and select those you find most appealing. Some of our personal choices are illustrated here. Prominent names include *Aporocactus, Astrophytum, Chamaecereus, Notocactus, Echinocereus, Opuntia,* Christmas poinsettia *(E. pulcherrima). Echinopsis, Gymnocalycium, Rebutia, Lobivia* and *Mammillaria.*

Indoors, these all need as much direct sun as you can give them. Outdoors, they can take all-day sun, or as little as a half day. To maintain indoors in a dim place, spotlight them with incandescent floodlights placed 4 feet away and burned 14 hours daily.

Aloe

These are easily cultivated succulent members of the Lily Family. Some like *A. aristata* stay ground-hugging rosettes for so long that they can be considered miniatures and others, like the true *Aloe vera*, have individual leaves up to 24 inches long. Good small kinds for pots and planters: *Aloe variegata, A. humilis* and *A. brevifolia*. Larger kinds: *A. vera, A. ciliaris, A. striata* and *A. arborescens.*

Agave

This famous succulent belongs to the Amaryllis Family. The true century plant, *Agave americana*, is too large for most container gardens except while it is young. Better for long-term pot growing: *A. americana* varieties *medio-picta* and *marginata, A. miradorensis, A. pumila* and *A. victoriae-reginae*. These dramatic rosette plants are great accents placed on patios, terraces, steps or balconies.

Crassula

There are hundreds of these, treasured for shape, color and growth habit. Most will bloom in season when provided warmth and sunlight. Indoors and outdoors, in pots, baskets and dish garden desertscapes, crassulas grow easily and well. Fluorescent-light culture okay also.

Succulent plantings can be fun. Terracotta tribal women don headdresses of grafted cactus and Euphorbia flanagani. *A crested cactus blends into the tough hide of the prehistoric looking armadillo. Velvety leaves of Kalanchoe beharensis are complimented by the clay woven basket.*

Echeveria

As a rule these hen-and-chickens succulents make geometrically perfect rosettes of leaves close to the ground; some look like glorious green roses. Grow in pots, pottery strawberry jars or all around big hanging, moss-stuffed wire balls. There are lots of species and hybrids. Recommended: *crenulata, derenbergii, elegans, multicaulis, pulvinata.*

Euphorbia

Weird and wonderful are these succulent relatives of the Christmas poinsettia (*E. pulcherrima*). Most popular: crown-of-thorns (*E. splendens*). For big, bold accents: cowhorn (*E. grandicornis*), hatrack (*E. lactea*) and pencil-cactus (*E. tirucalli*). Fascinating: Medusa's head (*E. caput-medusae*), green crown (*E. flanaganii*) and *E. biplurifolia.* red milk bush (*Synadenium*).

Kalanchoe

These succulents are closely related to echeveria; both are in the Crassula Family. Some are grown primarily for interesting foliage: *tomentosa, marmorata, tubiflora, pinnata* (baby plants form in the air on old leaves) and treelike *beharensis*. Others, especially *blossfeldiana* (and its named varieties like 'Tom Thumb,' 'Vulcan' and 'Brilliant Star'), *flammea* and *uniflora*, are cultivated for cherry, orange-red, apricot or yellow flowers (which come, incidentally, after the buds have been initiated by the shortest days of the year).

Sedum

There are hundreds of these you'd enjoy growing in containers. Our favorites include *pachyphyllum* (jelly bean), *treleasei, rubrotinctum, stahlii, dasyphyllum* (miniature creeper) and *multiceps* (little Joshua tree). A stellar basket plant is *morganianum;* shield it from wind and broiling sun; likes moist atmosphere.

Stapelia

These succulents are sometimes called carrion-fly plants because their

A. Ruffled Echeveria crenulata, *B. Giant specimen* Pachycereus pringlei, *C.* Kalanchoe beharensis, *D.* Echeveria elegans, *E.* Lithops bella *(living stones)*, *F.* Beaucarnea recurvata *(pony-tail palm)*, *G.* Espostoa lanata, *H.* Sempervivum tectorum *in owl planter*, *I. Golden barrel* Echinocactus grusonii *and J.* Ferocactus acanthodes.

flowers have an odor that tricks flies into thinking there is a dead animal there. Despite this odor, the stapelias have such fantastic, star-shaped flowers, that many people tolerate them, odor and all. They need summer shade, winter sun. *S. gigantea* has star flowers to 12 inches across diameter; *S. hirsuta* has 4-inch furry star flowers. *S. variegata* has 2-inch stars and less noticeable odor than others.

Stone plants

These incredible little succulent bodies seem to belong to the Mineral Kingdom. Collect species of *Lophophora*, *Lithops*, *Dinteranthus*, *Pleiospilos* and *Conophytum*, then have fun searching for look-alike stones to place in pots with them. Can be grown indoors or outdoors, also in fluorescent-lighted gardens. Some have daisylike flowers.

Wax plant

Leaves and fragrant flowers of *Hoya* are thick and waxy. Great basket and vine plants. Cuttings grow easily for long periods in water. Choicest are variegated forms of *H. carnosa* and miniature *H. bella*.

Windowed succulents

These wonders of nature, related to the stone plants, have translucent "window" areas in the top of each fat, clublike stem. One popular kind is *Fenestraria aurantiaca* which grows less than 2 inches tall. Some more common haworthias, such as *H. cymbiformis*, also have translucent leaf tips. Nature uses the "windows" to admit light to sand-covered plants.

Other succulents

Some of these are one-of-a-kind plants, others represent whole families you can have fun exploring. All thrive on pot culture, indoors and outdoors; all need frost-free winter quarters. These are commonly available: *Adromischus*, *Aeonium* (some like bronzy red-and-green roses), *Aptenia* (easy basket plant), *Beaucarnea* (pony-tail; an outstanding house plant), *Cotyledon*, *Faucaria* (tiger jaws), *Gasteria*, *Kleinia*, *Pedilanthus*, *Senecio rowleyanus* (string of pearls).

A. Euphorbia inermis, **B.** Agave expansa, **C.** Crassula *(African species)*, **D.** Kalanchoe tomentosa *(panda bear plant)*, **E.** Agave filifera, **F.** *Blooming* Rebutia, *collection*, **G.** Sedum *ground covering*, **H.** *Collection of* Euphorbia, **I.** Crassula falcata *and* **J.** *hanging basket of* Portulacaria afra variegata.

Try something new

The off-beat and the oddball plants . . . some beautiful, some interesting for what they do . . . all capture attention.

Unusual looking blooms of Anigozanthus.

In this category we find plants that are rarely grown by the container gardener along with new ideas for using horticultural materials or providing plant care.

A whole realm of things to grow, methods to grow them and ways to display them are available to the container gardener. The scope is as big as your imagination.

Be on constant lookout for something new to plant. Study seed and plant supplier catalogs. Read horticultural magazines to spark your imagination.

Whatever you choose to grow, these are the plants children love; all make good classroom projects.

African hemp

Large light green, translucent hairy leaves are characteristic of *Sparmannia africana*. This South African species grows treelike with woody stems. Winter-blooming large white flowers with yellow filaments are the size of hydrangeas. Keep in good light, out of direct sun, with lots of fresh air. Prune heavily after flowering

Fouquieria fasciculta is native to San Pedro Isle, Baja, California. This strange looking succulent stores water in the swollen woody base.

to keep the fast-growing plant held back for container gardening. Keep evenly moist.

Anigozanthus

This rare relative of the amaryllis is Australian in origin. Flowers may be scarlet, purple, yellow and white, or green with red markings as shown in *A. manglesii*. If you can locate an anigozanthus, propagate by division of roots in spring, or secure seeds from a rare seed specialist and plant in spring. Be prepared to wait about two years for blooms.

Apostle plant

Neomarica gracilis is the botanical name for this member of the Iris Family. It has delicate, small irislike flowers, white on the outside, blue in the throat, with a brown base. Common name comes from story that 12 leaves form before one turns brown. Place in a sunny location and keep wet.

Water lilies can bloom in very small pools.

Aquatics

Nothing makes a garden as cool as a pool of water with lush water plants. Use tubs, sawed-off barrels, concrete bowls or any other large containers of glass, plastic or wood. Sink the container into the earth or use them like any other pot. Water plants are easily grown, even indoors with ample sunlight.

Try horsetail *(Equisetum hyemale)*, Japanese iris *(Iris kaempferi)*, lotus *(Nelumbo)*, Cyperus, water-lilies and water-hyacinths. Many dwarf types of water plants are available for container pools.

Pot in fertilized loam and sink pots well below water level, or plant them in soil in the bottom of the container.

Try making an underwater garden in clear glass. This simple project is long-lasting and can be placed in areas with only artificial lighting. Buy little plants from a tropical fish store. Anchor them in a bed of fine gravel in the bottom of sparkling clean glass. Fill to top with water; change monthly.

Many foliage plants will grow in water (hydroponics). Remove all soil from their roots before placing them in a clear glass container. Put layers of gravel and sand to anchor the plants. Add a few small charcoal chips to keep water sweet. Use mild solution of liquid fertilizer in the water, keeping the container filled to the top. Change monthly.

Bamboo

Rapid growing bamboo adapts well to container gardening with good light, but must be protected from too much heat. A screen for privacy outdoors can be achieved by a series of tubs of bamboo making a living fence. The same idea works for indoor room dividers, but there should be alternate plants for rotation to outdoor environments. Keep bamboo moist.

Good bamboos for containers include *Phyllostachys nigra* (black-stemmed bamboo), *P. aurea* (golden bamboo), *Sasa palmata* (palmate bamboo) and *Bambusa multiplex riviereorum* (Chinese goddess bamboo). *B. nana* is a dwarf bamboo with light-green leaves and bluish reverses sparsely grown on dense, thin, hollow canes.

Bat-wing tree

Erythrina indica is a small tree with very thin, strong stems which are quite prickly. At the end of the stems are leaves resembling little green bats in flight. Red flowers and seed may be produced.

Begin your plant from seed. Nick sides of the hard covering and soak until seeds swell. Sow seed as instructed on pages 23-25. Germination takes up to 25 days. Keep soil damp.

Bonsai

This is an artistic form of container gardening, popular today in America because of the tremendous Oriental influence apparent in our lives. For centuries, Oriental gardeners have carefully, ever so patiently, trained trees into picturesque shapes, dwarfing them all the while so that a 100-year-old pine may live on the meager soil contained by a tray 6 inches x 12 inches x 2 inches deep.

Two examples of the ancient art of bonsai. The tree at the top is over 100 years old.

The art of growing bonsai requires an entire text. There are several outstanding books available on this subject. You will find firms which specialize in bonsai plants and supplies.

The busy gardener can make "instant" or "fake" bonsai by using rapid-growing tropical shrubs or trees. Select ones with small leaves and flowers. Follow the same technical procedures as for real bonsai, except much quicker as the trees grow all year. Give a warm, sunny, moist environment.

Cabbage and kale

The colorful, textured foliage of ornamental cabbages and flowering kale make beautiful container plants. Start them from seed in the summer or fall or purchase plants from garden centers or florists. Cabbages come in rich hues of purple and pink as well as many variations of white, cream and lavender. Kale produces tall spikes of tiny yellow blooms.

Not a giant rose, but a cabbage head.

Children's workshop

One of your most rewarding tasks as a gardener is to invite a group of youngsters into your home or garden and stimulate them to an appreciation for the wonder of nature. Your own children, the neighborhood gang or a classroom will find the gardening experience a fascinating new hobby. Show them how to sow seed, cultivate the earth, basics of container gardening and watch them try their hands at new ideas. Choose projects that are completed quickly; grow plants that do something (root vegetables, sprouts, morning-glories, venus fly-traps, sensitive plant, voodoo lilies). Children are fascinated by botanical names of plants and this is the time to learn to use and pronounce them. Make the entire experience fun and experimental. Let them discover for themselves the magical secrets of plant life.

Clematis

Spectacular flowers and beautiful vinelike foliage of many species of clematis can be grown indoors to provide blankets of color in almost every hue. Pot in moist soil enriched with leafmold and sweetened with lime. Keep in full sun, but keep the roots cool by mulching the top of the pot, or by placing pot within a larger pot as shown on page 12.

Spectacular flower of Clematis *vine.*

Cup-and-saucer-vine

Here's a showy climber to festoon a sunny or semisunny location indoors in spring, summer and fall. In late winter, plant several of the seeds in a 6- to 10-inch pot. Use a mixture of equal parts soil, sand and peat moss; keep this moist. As soon as possible, thin to the strongest plant or two in the pot. Fertilize biweekly as for other house plants. Vine will mature by early summer and produce an abundance of delightful violet and green cup-and-saucer flowers. Discard after one year and start anew from seeds. Known botanically as *Cobaea scandens.*

Shade loving blooms of flowering tobacco.

Flowering tobacco

Nicotiana alata grandiflora is a dwarf tobacco plant. The tender perennial bears many tubular blossoms, as shown above, towering over the small, dark green, hairy foliage. Flowers range from pink through maroon, green or brown to white. Unlike most flowering plants, nicotiana needs some shade. The little flowers will close on very sunny days and re-open again in the evening. Begin your plants from seed and water freely.

Found planters

Be on the lookout for unique, attractive objects to use as containers. It's usually best to use only a couple of such unusual planters in a collection in order to make them more outstanding. At the top of the next page we show use of a rock with a natural hollow, perfect for a succulent and a hollowed out part of a tree trunk growing with rosemary. Pick the trash—chances are you'll discover something you never imagined as a planter.

Planters made from stone and tree bark are great containers for Echeveria *and* Rosemary.

Gerbera

Sometimes called "African daisies" in honor of their native habitat, these are exquisite, daisylike flowers in delicate pastels and many vivid colors. It's best to buy transplants from the garden center. Indoors they bloom throughout the winter, and continue to bloom outdoors in warm climes through spring and into summer. Give the plants as much sun as possible, soak and allow to get almost dry, soak again.

Brightly colored Gerbera *or African daisy.*

Ginger

Add the aromatic tropical herbs to your container garden for lovely foliage and unusual, colorful flowers. Start as many species and varieties as possible. *Amonum cardamon* produces conelike yellow flower spikes among dark green lance-shaped leaves. *Costus* gingers have leaves growing like spiral staircases on the

stems. Brilliant orange flowers with ragged petals are produced.

Try *Curcuma roscoeana* for large spikes of concave orange bracts from which emerge shy yellow blooms. The "ginger-lilies" are *Hedychium* with beautiful large leaves and flowers with heady fragrances in pale yellow, brilliant red or white.

Kaempferia decora is a showy summer-bloomer with primrose-

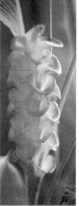

Ginger species come in many forms. Upper photo is Hedychium. *Below is* Amomum *and* Curcuma *in bloom.*

yellow flowers against cannalike leaves.

The commercial ginger root is from *Zingiber* with scented foliage in glossy green or variegated. Bright red spike flowers resembling pine cones are produced in the fall.

Most gingers are grown from tubers or corms and need moisture during growing season, drying off during their dormant period.

Honeybells

This plant is seldom seen, but deserves to be better known. It has fragrant golden, pendant flowers in winter and spring; known botanically as *Mahernia verticillata*. A good pot plant for a sunny window sill. Besides a sunny position in winter, provide moderate warmth (preferably with no long periods of more than 70° in winter).

Insectivorous plants

These are among the most interesting subjects in the entire plant kingdom; instead of taking their nourishment from the soil, and surrounding air, they trap insects by various ingenious devices. They are difficult house plants, but worth a try in some kind of terrarium. Children find these strange plants fascinating. As a group project, ask your local drive-in or hospital kitchen to save gallon pickle jars and lids for you. These make perfect planting containers for insectivorous plants. Screwed in place, the lids assure constant moisture inside, but punch holes in them if you add live insects. The Venus flytrap *(Dionaea muscipula)*, and cobra plant *(Darlingtonia californica)* are frequently offered by mail-order houses.

Provide coolness, preferably a temperature range of 45 to 65° and sun to semishade.

Jatropha

The unusual looking plant shown below is a member of the Euphorbia family. Water can be stored for long periods in the bulb portion. Jatrophas have a milky juice, usually poisonous. Some species grow naturally in Southern California and Florida.

Barbados nut tree *(J. curcas)* blooms with clusters of yellow-green flowers. Seed fruits look like dark red olives. Foliage is maple-like.

The peregrina nettlespurge *(J. hastata)* is native to Cuba. Many red flowers are produced against oblong leaves. *J. multifida* is known as coral plant with rounded leaves with deep-cut lobes and clusters of red flowers.

Jatropha berlandieri, an unusual euphorbia.

Kitchen garden

In our age of recycling don't throw away those food scraps—make a garden out of them. These projects have much appeal to children, but can be interesting to any container gardener.

CARROT TOPS make interesting plants. Take a large carrot with some of the leaf tips still showing on the end. Cut off the slimmer part of the root, until the carrot has a length of 2 to 3 inches. Hollow out the bottom end; make two holes on opposite sides and put a decorative cord or string through these. Hang the carrot in a bright window. Fill the hollowed-out part with water, and re-fill as often as necessary to keep moisture there. Soon the leaves will begin to sprout out of the lower part, making an unusual plant. It will last several weeks; then discard.

Sprouts of beans and oats make lovely saucer gardens. Clip seedlings for salads.

AVOCADO seeds sprout readily and grow into attractive, leafy plants. Insert three toothpicks in the broad end of the seed; these will hold it over the top of a glass of water filled so that the base of the seed just rests in the moisture. Set the glass in a bright window, and keep the water level constant. In time you will see roots form, then a green sprout. Eventually, you will need to transplant the young avocado to a pot of equal parts soil, sand and peat moss; keep this moist. Pinching out the growing tip of the young plant will encourage it to branch.

SWEET POTATOES root readily when placed half in and half out of a container of water. Look for one with sprouts showing; many sweet potatoes sold at the supermarket have been treated so that they will not sprout. Until the potato vine gets too large, change the water once a week, pouring out the old and replacing with new; a few chunks of charcoal in the container will help keep the water fresh. Sweet potato vines will climb a small trellis indoors, grow as hanging basket plants, or as vine to trail over a table or cabinet top.

PINEAPPLE TOPS can be rooted in water or planted in soil to base of leaves and grown as a bromeliad.

CITRUS SEED planted in small pots produce miniature trees.

Leopard plant

Ligularia tussilaginea aureo-maculata is the botanical appendage for this member of the Daisy Family. Surprisingly enough, it is grown for a rosette of long-stemmed, leathery leaves, attractively spotted with gold, and quite un-daisylike. Provide semisun to semishade, and a cool place in winter (62 to 72° is good). Pot in a mixture of equal parts soil, sand, peat moss; keep this evenly moist.

Night-blooming jessamine

Cestrum nocturnum is a gangly tropical shrub with oval green leaves and small tubular white flowers, extremely fragrant in the evening. Blooms appear off and on through the year. *C. parqui* has willowlike leaves, black berries and green-white nightly fragrant flowers. Keep pinched back for bushy growth. It may be necessary to stake for support. Give it good light and keep evenly moist. In addition to the night bloomers there are varieties that flower with daytime fragrances.

Peanuts

The strange growing habits of peanuts make them an interesting plant to grow, especially in clear glass or plastic where you can observe their activity. Bright yellow flowers are produced in the usual way, but as they fade a peg forms at the stem end and bends down to the soil. This thrusts the seed into the earth where it becomes a nut. Use a light soil mix. When leaves die back pull up plant and hang to dry peanuts.

Pregnant Onion

The common name for *Ornithogalum caudatum* comes from its habit of producing so many offsprings—as many as 40 per year. The green bulb is planted mostly on top of the soil. Germination will occur in ten days under fluorescent lights. Tiny bulbs are produced on sides of the parent. Flowers of lavender or yellow-white are produced in clusters at the end of long stems.

Radar Plant

A nervous little tri-leafed plant with insignificant flowers and jointed seed

Ornithogalum caudatum is the pregnant onion or German-flower, a prolific bulb.

pods, *Desmodium gyrans* never stops turning in the sunlight. The leaves continually point in different directions. Grow this curious annual from seed and keep in a sunny place.

Redwood Burl

Sequoia sempervirens comes to you as a knotty brown burl cut from the trunks of the oldest living trees on earth—the California redwoods. When placed in a shallow dish of water, tiny specks of green appear. Never allow the dish to dry out. Keep out of bright sun and watch lush green, fernlike foliage develop. The plant lasts indefinitely. Sometimes the sprouts will root and these can be planted in pots. Don't expect a giant redwood, but it can produce a nice miniature tree which you can keep for years.

Redwood burl in its native habitat. Cut and placed in water, it makes a lovely plant.

Resurrection Plant

Selaginella lepidophylla is a native to deserts from Texas to South America. It has the ability to assume an appearance of death when denied water. The dainty foliage curls into a crackly, brownish ball-like mass. When given moisture, it unfolds and green growth appears. Resurrection plant can be dried again, kept on a dry shelf for indefinite periods of time. Start growth again merely by placing in water. A similar acting plant is *Anastatica*. Another is a fern, *Polypodium polypodioides*, whose fronds curl inward when dry, then unfold when moisture is available.

Rootview Box

Construct a box of marine plywood with drainage holes and one side of clear plastic or plate glass, with a panel to cover during germination. Plant seeds or seedlings and watch how plants develop and roots grow. It's good for experimenting with effects of soils and fertilizer.

Root view box exposes miracle of growth.

Sea Onion

This strange plant is grown more for curiosity than for beauty. It has a succulent green bulb, most of which is below ground. From this there grows a long plume of bright green foliage which needs a trellis support. Known botanically as *Bowiea volubilis,* and sometimes called climbing onion.

Sensitive plant

This is known botanically as *Mimosa pudica*. It is a weak-branched little plant with wicked thorns, and airy, ferny foliage which winces at the slightest touch; children of all ages love to tease it. Small plants are often available at local greenhouses, and always by mail from house-plant specialists. Or, you can plant the seeds in moist soil; keep them in warmth to encourage quick sprouting.

Shoo-fly plant

This is known botanically as *Nicandra physalodes,* a member of the Nightshade Family (tomatoes and peppers are related). It is said to repel flies. The blue and white flowers appear in summer. Plant seeds in early spring; transplant singly or by threes to 6- or 7-inch pots of a mixture of equal parts soil, sand and peat moss; keep this moist. Pinch back the stems frequently until midsummer to encourage bushiness.

Shower trees

This common name for *Cassia* comes from the dripping cascade of pink or yellow flowers at the end of its branches. The herb senna is produced by the tree which is Mexican in origin. Plants may be propagated from seed, but expect a long wait.

Topiary

This is a process where plants are trained or pruned into unnatural shapes. Such plants are commonplace in formal gardens. An amusing touch to your container garden can be added by one of these stronglyshaped plants. Shrubs like boxwood can be pruned to produce desired shapes.

Wire frames are available on which vines and creepers can be tied to make almost any shape. Try using ivy

Topiary can take many forms with a little aid from wire frames and careful pruning.

or *Ficus pumila*. Plant several long trailers in a pot, anchor the frame (make your own from heavy wire, if commercial ones aren't available) in the center and tie vines to the wire with green thread or twist-em.

Voodoo plant

Also called snake palm and devil's tongue, this plant is a calla-lily relative known botanically as *Hydrosme rivieri*.

The tubers of the voodoo plant can be potted in a mixture of equal parts soil, sand and peat moss; keep this evenly moist. Like its calla-lily relatives, this plant thrives on lots of water and sunlight while it is in growth. In the winter or spring the large tubers send up bloom spikes. The giant reddish black blossom is completely unlike anything you've ever seen before in the plant kingdom; the spathe which projects out of the flowerlike spadix smells of carrion. This spathe, a fingerlike growth, gives the plant its "devil's tongue" name. If this is cut out as soon as the bloom opens, the plant will not smell so obnoxious.

After blooming, voodoo plant sends up a magnificent fanlike umbrella of foliage atop a thick, snake-spotted stem. When the weather warms up, the voodoo may be planted outdoors in a part of the garden protected from strong winds. The foliage lasts until frost. Then dig the tubers and store them in a mouseproof place in coolness (50 to 65°). In early winter, pot the tubers and begin the cycle anew.

Walking iris

Neomarica northiana has small irislike flowers and gets its common name because bloom stems bend to earth after flowering, root into the moist surface and send up new plants. Obviously, if grown outdoors in a favorable climate, it would "walk." Place in a brightly lighted area and keep wet at all times. Let tips of bloom stems root in pot of moist soil, then cut from mother plant.

Yesterday, today and tomorrow

This is the picturesque, but appropriate name for *Brunfelsia calycina floribunda*, a shrubby plant which may be grown in an 8- to 10-inch pot or tub indoors. From early winter to midsummer the plants bear quantities of 2-inch flowers. These open dark violet, change to lilac and finally fade to white—hence "yesterday, today and tomorrow."

Mini-encyclopedia of house plants

COMMON NAME	BOTANICAL NAME	SOIL MIX					LIGHT				WATER				TEMPERATURE			HUMIDITY			PROPAGATION
		All purpose	High Humus	Gritty lean	Loose medium	High acid	Sunny	Semi-sunny	Semi-shady	Shady	Keep wet at all times	Keep evenly moist	Approach dryness between waterings	Let dry out between waterings	Cool	Average house	Warm	Very moist	Moist	Average house	
Acalypha	*Acalypha*	●						●	●			●				●				●	Cuttings in fall
Achimenes	*Achimenes*		●					●	●			●				●				●	Rhizome division, seed, stem cuttings
Acorus	*Acorus*	●							●		●				●			●			Division in spring or fall
African hemp	*Sparmannia africana*	●						●				●				●				●	Cuttings
African violet	*Saintpaulia*		●					●	●			●				●			●		Seed, leaf cuttings, division
Agapanthus	*Agapanthus*	●					●	●	●			●			●	●				●	Division in early spring
Allamanda	*Allamanda*	●						●				●				●			●		Cuttings of half-ripened stems in spring
Amaryllis	*Hippeastrum*		●					●	●			●				●				●	Remove offsets at potting time; sow spring seed
Anemone	*Anemone*	●					●	●				●			●						Seed or offsets
Anigozanthus	*Anigozanthus*	●					●					●			●					●	Seed or root division
Anthurium	*Anthurium*				●				●			●					●	●			Cuttings or offsets
Apostle plant	*Neomarica gracilis*	●						●	●			●				●				●	Division of rhizomes
Aralia	*Dizygotheca elegantissima*, also see: *Polyscias* and *Fatsia*		●					●	●			●				●				●	Cuttings
Ardisia	*Ardisia*	●						●	●			●			●					●	Seed or cuttings
Asparagus fern	*Asparagus*	●						●	●	●		●				●				●	Seed or clump division
Aspidistra	*Aspidistra*	●						●	●	●		●				●				●	Division of roots in late winter or spring
Aucuba	*Aucuba japonica*	●						●	●			●				●				●	Seed or cuttings
Azalea	*Azalea*	●				●	●	●				●				●			●		Stem cuttings
Baby's-tears	*Helxine*		●						●	●		●				●			●		Division of clumps or cuttings
Bamboo	*Bambusa*		●					●	●			●				●			●	●	Division of large clumps
Bat-wing tree	*Erythrina indica*	●						●	●			●				●				●	Seed
Begonia	*Begonia rex; Begonia semperflorens*; Rhizomatous species; Fibrous-rooted, cane species; Tuberous-rooted species; and Fibrous-rooted species		●					●	●	●			●				●			●	●	Cuttings or seed
Bird-of-Paradise	*Strelitzia*	●						●	●			●			●					●	Division of rhizomes, remove suckers in spring
Bougainvillea	*Bougainvillea*	●						●				●				●			●		Seed in spring or cuttings of half-ripe wood
Bromeliad:	*Aechmea*			●				●	●				●			●				●	Remove offsets
Pineapple	*Ananas*		●					●	●				●			●			●		Root top of fruit
	Billbergia			●				●	●				●			●				●	Detach suckers
Earth stars	*Cryptanthus*		●					●	●				●			●				●	Remove offsets
	Neoregelia			●				●	●				●			●				●	Detach suckers
Living vase or Flaming-sword	*Vriesia*		●					●	●				●			●			●		Remove suckers or plantlets
Brassaia (Schefflera)	*Brassaia*	●					●	●	●	●		●					●			●	Cuttings of half-ripened stems

COMMON NAME	BOTANICAL NAME	SOIL MIX					LIGHT				WATER				TEMPERATURE			HUMIDITY			PROPAGATION
		All purpose	High Humus	Gritty lean	Loose medium	High acid	Sunny	Semi-sunny	Semi-shady	Shady	Keep wet at all times	Keep evenly moist	Approach dryness between waterings	Let dry out between waterings	Cool	Average house	Warm	Very moist	Moist	Average house	
Cactus:	Aporocactus; Astrophytum; Cephalocereus; Chamaecereus; Cleistocactus Echinocactus; Echinocereus; Echinopsis; Gymnocalycium; Lobivia; Mammillaria; Notocactus; Opuntia; Pereskia; Rebutia;			•			•	•						•		•				•	Offsets or cuttings
	Ephiphyllum; Hylocereus; Selenicereus;	•						•	•			•				•			•		Cuttings in spring or summer
	Schlumbergera; and Zygocactus	•						•	•			•				•			•		Cuttings
Caladium	Caladium	•						•	•			•					•		•		Divide tubers or clumps in spring
Calceolaria	Calceolaria	•						•	•	•		•			•				•		Seed in April or August
Calla-lily	Zantedeschia	•						•			•					•			•		Seed or offsets
Camellia	Camellia japonica		•			•	•	•				•			•			•			Cuttings of current season's new wood
Chinese evergreen	Aglaonema	•						•	•	•		•				•				•	Root stems
Chlorophytum (spider)	Chlorophytum	•						•	•	•		•				•				•	Remove aerial plantlets or division
Chrysanthemum	Chrysanthemum	•						•	•			•			•					•	Cuttings
Cineraria	Senecio cruentus	•						•	•			•			•				•		Seed in summer
Citrus	Citrus	•						•	•			•				•				•	Cuttings of half-ripened wood in spring
Clematis	Clematis		•					•				•				•				•	Seed, layering, division, cuttings, or grafting
Clerodendrum	Clerodendrum		•					•	•			•				•				•	Cuttings of half-ripened wood or remove suckers
Clivia	Clivia	•						•	•			•			•	•				•	Division
Cobra plant	Darlingtonia californica		•	•				•	•	•		•				•			•		Seed or shoots in summer
Coccoloba (Seagrape)	Coccoloba	•						•	•			•				•				•	Seed, layering, wood cuttings
Coffee	Coffea	•						•	•		•				•	•			•		Seed or wood cuttings
Coleus	Coleus blumei	•					•	•				•				•				•	Seed or stem cuttings
Columnea	Columnea		•					•	•			•				•		•			Tip cuttings or seed
Creeping Charlie	Pilea nummularifolia (also see: Plectranthus)		•					•	•			•				•				•	Cuttings
Creeping fig	Ficus pumila or Fradicans	•						•	•	•		•				•				•	Cuttings
Crossandra	Crossandra		•					•				•				•			•		Seed or tip cuttings
Croton	Codiaeum		•				•	•				•				•			•		Cuttings
Cup-and-saucer vine	Cobaea scandens	•					•	•				•				•				•	Seed
Cyclamen	Cyclamen		•					•	•			•			•				•		Seed
Cyperus	Cyperus	•						•		•	•				•				•		Division

COMMON NAME	BOTANICAL NAME	SOIL MIX					LIGHT				WATER				TEMPERATURE			HUMIDITY			PROPAGATION
		All purpose	High Humus	Gritty lean	Loose medium	High acid	Sunny	Semi-sunny	Semi-shady	Shady	Keep wet at all times	Keep evenly moist	Approach dryness between waterings	Let dry out between waterings	Cool	Average house	Warm	Very moist	Moist	Average house	
Cycas fern or palm	Cycas	•						•				•				•				•	Seed or dormant suckers
Dieffenbachia (Dumb cane)	Dieffenbachia	•						•	•	•			•			•				•	Stem cuttings or layering
Dipladenia	Dipladenia splendens	•					•	•				•				•		•			Stem cuttings or seed
Dracaena	Dracaena	•						•	•	•		•				•				•	Stem cuttings, layering, root division
	Pleomele	•						•	•	•		•				•				•	Stem cuttings, layering, root division
Easter lily	Lilium longiflorum	•						•					•		•					•	Plant bulbs
Euonymus	Euonymus	•						•	•			•			•				•		Cuttings of half-ripened wood in fall or winter
Elaeagnus	Elaeagnus	•						•	•			•			•	•			•		Cuttings in spring
Fatshedera	Fatshedera lizei	•					•	•	•			•			•	•			•		Cuttings
Fatsia	Fatsia japonica		•					•				•			•	•			•		Cuttings of branches
Ferns: Bird's-nest	Asplenium		•					•	•			•			•				•		Remove offsets or root plantlets
Boston or sword	Nephrolepis		•					•	•			•				•				•	Division of clumps
Bear's-paw	Polypodium		•					•	•			•				•				•	Division of clumps
Holly	Cyrtomium		•					•	•			•			•				•		Rhizome division
Maidenhair	Adiantum		•		•			•	•	•		•				•			•		Division of clumps
Miniature	Polystichum		•						•			•				•				•	Division
Rabbit's-foot	Davallia		•						•			•			•				•		Rhizome division
Staghorn	Platycerium				•			•	•			•				•			•		Remove offsets
Table or brake	Pteris		•						•			•			•				•		Division
Ficus or fig	Ficus	•						•	•	•		•				•				•	Air layering
Fittonia	Fittonia		•					•	•			•			•				•		Tip cuttings
Flame violet	Episcia		•					•	•			•					•		•		Root stolens
Flowering maple	Abutilon	•					•					•				•				•	Stem cuttings
Flowering tobacco	Nicotiana	•						•	•		•					•				•	Seed
Fragrant gladiolus	Acidanthera	•					•					•				•				•	New corms in spring
Freesia	Freesia	•					•					•			•				•		Seed or offsets
Fuchsia	Fuchsia	•					•	•				•			•				•		Cuttings in spring
Gardenia	Gardenia	•			•	•	•					•				•			•		Cuttings of half-ripened wood
Gerbera	Gerbera	•					•	•				•				•				•	
Geranium	Pelargonium	•					•	•						•	•	•			•	•	Cuttings
Ginger:	Amomum	•						•	•			•				•				•	Clump division
Spiral	Costus		•					•	•			•				•			•		Clump division in spring
	Curcuma		•					•	•			•				•		•			Division of tubers in spring
Ginger lilies	Hedychium	•						•			•	•				•			•		Division of tubers at rest time
Peacock plant	Kaempferia		•					•	•			•				•			•		Seed or clump division
Commercial ginger root	Zingiber		•					•	•			•				•			•		Division of clumps in spring
Gloriosa	Gloriosa rothschildiana	•					•	•				•				•			•		Seed or tuber division
Gloxinia	Sinningia	•						•				•				•			•		Seed, leaf or stem cuttings, tuber division

COMMON NAME	BOTANICAL NAME	SOIL MIX					LIGHT				WATER				TEMPERA-TURE			HUMIDITY			PROPAGATION
		All purpose	High Humus	Gritty lean	Loose medium	High acid	Sunny	Semi-sunny	Semi-shady	Shady	Keep wet at all times	Keep evenly moist	Approach dryness between waterings	Let dry out between waterings	Cool	Average house	Warm	Very moist	Moist	Average house	
Gynura	*Gynura*	●					●					●				●				●	Cuttings
Haemanthus	*Haemanthus*	●						●	●			●				●			●		Remove offsets when repotting
Hawaiian ti	*Cordyline terminalis*	●						●	●	●	●					●				●	Stem cutting, layering, root division
Hibiscus	*Hibiscus*	●					●					●				●			●		Stem cuttings
Homalomena	*Homalomena*	●							●	●		●				●			●		Stem cuttings
Hydrangea	*Hydrangea*	●				●	●	●			●	●			●					●	Stem cuttings
Hypoestes	*Hypoestes*		●					●	●			●				●			●		Seed or cuttings
Impatiens	*Impatiens*	●						●	●	●			●			●		●			Cuttings
Iresine	*Iresine*	●					●						●		●	●				●	Cuttings
Ivy, English	*Hedera helix*	●					●	●	●	●		●	●		●	●			●	●	Cuttings
Ixia	*Ixia*	●					●						●	●		●			●		Bulb offsets
Ixora	*Ixora*	●						●	●					●		●			●		Strong cuttings
Jatropha	*Jatropha*	●						●	●			●				●			●	●	Seed or cuttings
Jerusaleum cherry	*Solanum*	●						●	●			●			●				●		Seed
Jessamine, night-blooming	*Cestrum nocturnum*		●					●	●			●			●					●	Cuttings
Joseph's coat	*Alternanthera*	●						●	●			●				●				●	Cuttings
King's crown	*Jacobina carnea*	●						●				●				●			●		Cuttings
Leopard plant	*Ligularia tussilaginea*	●							●	●		●			●					●	Dividing plants with more than one crown
Liriope or lily turf	*Ophiopogon*	●							●	●		●			●				●		Division
Lipstick vine	*Aeschynanthus*		●	●				●	●			●				●			●		Stem or tip cuttings
Miniature rose	*Rosa*	●					●	●				●				●			●		Seed or cuttings
Montbretia	*Crocosmia*	●					●					●				●				●	Seed or offsets
Myrtle	*Myrtus communis*	●					●	●					●		●					●	Cuttings of ripened wood
Nandina	*Nandina*	●						●	●			●				●				●	Stem cuttings
Norfolk Island pine	*Araucaria excelsa*	●						●	●			●			●	●				●	Seed or root tops of old plants
Oleander	*Nerium oleander*	●					●	●				●				●			●		Cuttings of firm tip growth in spring or summer
Orchid:	*Brassavola*				●		●	●						●		●		●			Division in late winter
	Cattleya				●		●	●						●		●		●			Division in late winter
Swan	*Cycnoches*	●						●	●			●				●		●			Division in spring or summer
	Epidendrum				●			●	●				●			●		●			Air layering or division in spring
Tiger	*Odontoglossum*				●				●						●	●		●			Division in spring or summer
Butterfly	*Oncidium*				●			●	●			●				●		●			Division in spring
Lady slipper	*Paphiopedilum*				●				●			●				●		●			Division in spring
Dogwood or moth	*Phalaenopsis*				●			●	●			●				●		●			Division in spring
Oxalis	*Oxalis*	●					●	●				●				●			●		Offsets or division
Palms: Bamboo	*Chamaedorea*	●							●	●		●				●				●	Seed or remove suckers
Butterfly	*Chrysalidocarpus*	●						●	●			●				●				●	Seed or clump division in spring

Common Name	Botanical Name	Soil: All purpose	Soil: High Humus	Soil: Gritty lean	Soil: Loose medium	Soil: High acid	Light: Sunny	Light: Semi-sunny	Light: Semi-shady	Light: Shady	Water: Keep wet at all times	Water: Keep evenly moist	Water: Approach dryness between waterings	Water: Let dry out between waterings	Temp: Cool	Temp: Average house	Temp: Warm	Humidity: Very moist	Humidity: Moist	Humidity: Average house	Propagation
Date	*Phoenix*	•							•	•		•				•				•	Seed or remove suckers
Fan	*Chamaerops*	•						•	•		•	•			•					•	Seed or suckers
	Licuala	•							•	•		•				•			•		Seed or suckers
	Livistona	•							•	•		•				•			•		Seed or suckers
	Rhapis	•							•	•		•			•					•	Seed or suckers
Fishtail	*Caryota*	•						•	•			•				•				•	Seed in March
Pandanus	*Pandanus*		•				•	•				•				•		•			Remove suckers
Passion flower	*Passiflora*		•				•	•				•				•				•	Seed or cuttings
Pellionia	*Pellionia*	•							•	•		•				•			•		Cuttings
Peperomia	*Peperomia*	•						•	•	•			•			•				•	Stem or leaf cuttings
Philodendron	*Philodendron*	•						•	•	•		•				•			•	•	Stem cuttings or offsets
Pilea (Artillery, Aluminum, Moon Valley)	*Pilea*		•						•			•				•			•	•	Cuttings
Pittosporum	*Pittosporum*	•						•	•			•			•				•		Cuttings of half-ripened wood
Plectranthus (Swedish ivy)	*Plectranthus*	•						•	•	•		•				•				•	Seed or stem cuttings
Podocarpus	*Podocarpus*	•							•			•			•				•		Seed or ripened wood cuttings
Polyscias	*Polyscias*	•					•	•	•	•		•			•	•			•		Cuttings
Prayer plant	*Maranta*		•						•			•				•			•		Division
Pregnant onion	*Ornithogalum caudatum*	•						•						•		•				•	Remove offsets
Primrose	*Primula*		•					•	•			•			•				•		Seed
Privet	*Ligustrum*	•					•	•				•				•				•	Stem cuttings
Pyracantha	*Pyracantha*	•					•					•			•					•	Soft wood cuttings in early summer
Radar plant	*Desmondium gyrans*	•					•					•				•				•	Seed in February
Ranunculus	*Ranunculus*	•					•					•			•				•		Seed in March; roots in autumn
Redwood burl	*Sequoia sempervirens*						•	•	•	•						•				•	Plantlets can be rooted
Resurrection plant	*Selaginella lepidophylla*						•	•	•	•						•				•	Purchase in dried form
Rhododendron	*Rhododendron*					•	•	•				•			•				•		Stem cuttings
Rhoeo (Moses-in-the-Cradle)	*Rhoeo*	•					•	•	•			•				•				•	Remove offset or transplant seedlings from parent
Rosary vine	*Ceropegia woodi*	•					•	•	•				•			•				•	Cuttings or plant bulblets along stems
Sansevieria	*Sansevieria*	•					•	•	•	•			•			•				•	Division of rootstock or leaf cuttings
Saxifraga	*Saxifraga*	•						•	•			•	•		•					•	Remove young plants
Scindapsus	*Scindapsus aureus*	•						•	•	•			•				•			•	Cuttings
Selaginella	*Selaginella*		•						•	•		•				•		•			Cuttings
Sensitive plant	*Mimosa pudica*	•					•	•	•	•		•				•			•		Seed or transplants
Shoo-fly plant	*Nicandra physalodes*	•					•	•				•				•				•	Seed
Shower plant	*Cassia*	•					•	•				•				•				•	Seed
Shrimp plant	*Beloperone guttata*	•					•	•					•			•			•		Cuttings
Spathiphyllum	*Spathiphyllum*		•					•	•			•					•		•		Division of rootstock

COMMON NAME	BOTANICAL NAME	SOIL MIX					LIGHT				WATER				TEMPERATURE			HUMIDITY			PROPAGATION
		All purpose	High Humus	Gritty lean	Loose medium	High acid	Sunny	Semi-sunny	Semi-shady	Shady	Keep wet at all times	Keep evenly moist	Approach dryness between waterings	Let dry out between waterings	Cool	Average house	Warm	Very moist	Moist	Average house	
Stephanotis	*Stephanotis floribunda*		•				•	•				•				•			•		Cuttings of half-mature stems in spring
Succulents: Century plant	*Agave*	•					•							•	•	•				•	Remove offsets
	Aloe	•					•	•				•				•				•	Seed or offsets
Ice plant	*Aptenia*	•					•					•				•				•	Stem cuttings
Pony-tail	*Beaucarnea*	•					•	•				•				•				•	Remove offset
	Bowiea	•						•	•			•			•					•	Remove offsets
Propeller, rattle-snake, scarlet paintbrush, etc.	*Crassula*	•					•	•				•	•			•				•	Seed or cuttings
	Eschiveria	•					•	•						•		•				•	Offsets or stem cuttings
Poinsettia, Crown-of thorns, etc.	*Euphorbia*	•					•	•				•				•				•	Cuttings
Tiger jaws	*Faucaria*			•			•							•		•				•	Seed or cuttings
Baby toes	*Fenestraria*			•			•							•		•				•	Seed or cuttings
Ox-tongue	*Gasteria*	•						•	•			•				•				•	Seed or offsets
Zebra or wart	*Haworthia*	•					•	•				•				•				•	Seed or offsets
	Kalanchoe	•					•	•						•	•	•	•			•	Potting plantlets, seed, or tip cuttings
Living stones, stone face	*Lithops*			•			•						•			•				•	Seed in spring
	Pachyveria	•					•	•						•		•				•	Offsets or stem cuttings
Devil's backbone	*Pedilanthus*	•					•	•				•				•				•	Cuttings in spring
Mistletoe cactus	*Rhipsalis*	•			•				•	•		•					•	•			Cuttings
	Scilla	•						•	•			•				•		•			Offsets in autumn
Donkey's tail, coral beads, etc.	*Sedum*	•					•	•						•	•	•				•	Seed, cuttings, or division
Starfish flower	*Stapelia*		•				•	•				•				•				•	Division or cuttings in late spring or summer
String-of-pearls	*Senecio rowleyanus*	•					•	•					•			•				•	
Sweet-olive	*Osmanthus fragrans*	•					•	•				•			•				•		Cuttings of half-ripened wood in summer
Tibouchina	*Tibouchina*	•						•	•				•		•				•		Cuttings
Tolmeia (Piggy-back)	*Tolmeia*		•						•	•		•			•						Pin baby plants into damp soil
Tulbaghia	*Tulbaghia*	•					•	•				•				•				•	Offsets in spring or fall
Voodoo plant	*Hydrosme rivieri*	•						•	•			•				•				•	Remove offsets from tuber
Walking iris	*Neomarica northiana*	•					•	•				•			•				•		From small plants formed by flowers
Wandering Jew	*Gibasis*	•					•	•	•			•			•				•		Cuttings anytime
	Setcreasea	•					•	•	•				•		•					•	Cuttings anytime
	Tradescantia	•					•	•	•				•		•					•	Cuttings anytime
	Zebrina	•					•	•	•			•				•			•		Cuttings anytime
Yesterday, Today and Tomorrow	*Bruntsfelsia calycina*	•						•				•				•			•		Cuttings
Zebra plant	*Aphelandra*	•						•				•				•			•		Tip cuttings in spring

Department of resources

Only a few years ago, most of us who wanted a container plant that was the least bit unusual had to send away for it from a specialist. Because of plant popularity and mass dissemination of rare species and new varieties, this is all changing today. More and more local garden centers and plant shops offer the choice, the offbeat, the truly exotic. However, there are certain special plants available only from highly specialized suppliers, and for that reason we list these growers here, along with mailing addresses and an indication of any changes made for catalogs. It is also true that some persons who live away from the population centers need to order all plants and supplies by mail.

Source for plants

ABBEY GARDEN
P.O. Box 30331, Santa Barbara, CA 93105
Cacti and other succulents. Catalog $1.00.

ABBOT'S NURSERY
Route 4, Box 482, Mobile, AL 36009
Camellias.

ALBERTS & MERKEL BROTHERS
P.O. Box 537, Boynton Beach, FL 33435
Orchids and other tropicals. Catalog $1.00.

ANTONELLI BROTHERS
2545 Capitola Road, Santa Cruz, CA 95010
Tuberous begonias, gloxinias, achimenes.

ASHCROFT ORCHIDS
19062 Ballinger Way N.E., Seattle 55, WA
Botanical orchids.

BART'S NURSERY
522 Fifth Street, Fullerton, PA
Bonsai materials.

BUELL, ALBERT H.
Eastford, CT 06242
African violets, gloxinias, other gesneriads. Catalog $1.00.

BURGESS SEED AND PLANT COMPANY
Galesburg, MI 49053
Dwarf fruit, other house plants.

BURNETT BROTHERS, INC.
92 Chambers Street, New York, NY 10007
Freesias and other bulbous plants.

BURPEE, W. ATLEE, COMPANY
Philadelphia, PA 19132; Clinton, IA 52733; and Riverside, CA 92502
Seeds, bulbs, supplies.

COOK'S GERANIUM NURSERY
712 North Grand, Lyons, KS 67544
Geraniums. Catalog 50¢.

CONARD PYLE STAR ROSES
West Grove, PA 19390
Miniature roses, clematis.

DE GIORGI COMPANY, INC.
Council Bluffs, IA 51504
Seeds and bulbs.

DE JAGER, P., AND SONS, INC.
188 Asbury Street, South Hamilton, MA 01982
Bulbs for forcing.

FARMER SEED AND NURSERY COMPANY
Faribault, MN 55021
Dwarf citrus and other house plants.

FENNELL ORCHID COMPANY
26715 S.W. 157 Avenue, Homestead, FL 33030
Orchids.

FIELD, HENRY, SEED AND NURSERY COMPANY
Shenandoah, IA 51601
House plants and supplies.

FISCHER GREENHOUSES
Linwood, NJ
African violets and other gesneriads; supplies for growing house plants.

FRENCH, J. HOWARD
Baltimore Pike, Lima, PA 19060
Bulbs for forcing.

GREEN ACRES NURSERY
14451 N.E. Second Street, North Miami, FL 33161
Palms.

HAUSERMANN'S ORCHIDS
Box 363, Elmhurst, IL 60128
Unusual species orchids.

HILLTOP FARM
Route 3, Box 216, Cleveland, TX
Geraniums and herbs.

HOWARD, S.M., ORCHIDS
Seattle Heights, WA 98063
Unusual orchids.

JONES AND SCULLY, INC.
2200 N.E. 33rd Avenue, Miami, FL 33142
Orchids and other tropicals.

KARTUZ, MICHAEL J.
92 Chestnut Street, Wilmington, MA 01887
House plants, many bred specifically for fluorescent-light culture. Catalog 50¢.

LOGEE'S GREENHOUSES
55 North Street, Danielson, CT 06239
All kinds of house plants including rare and unusual exotics. Catalog $1.00.

LYON, LYNDON
14 Mutchler Street, Dolgeville, NY 13329
African violets, gesneriads.

McCLELLAN, ROD, COMPANY
1450 El Camino Real,
South San Francisco, CA 94080
Orchids and supplies for growing.

MERRY GARDENS
Camden, ME 04843
Complete selection of house plants and herbs. Catalog $1.00.

MINI-ROSES
Box 4255 Station A, Dallas, TX 75208
Miniature roses.

NIES NURSERY
5710 S.W. 37th Street, West Hollywood, FL 33023
Palms.

NUCCIO'S NURSERIES
3555 Chaney Trail, Altadena, CA 91002
Camellias.

PARK, GEORGE W., SEED CO., INC.
Greenwood, SC 29647
All kinds of house plants, seeds, bulbs, fluorescent-lighting equipment, other supplies.

REASONER'S TROPICAL NURSERIES, INC.
P.O. Box 1881, Bradenton, FL
Tropicals.

RIVERMONT ORCHIDS
P.O. Box 67, Signal Mountain, TN
Orchids.

SEQUOIA NURSERY
2519 East Noble Avenue, Visalia, CA 93277
Miniature roses, including basket and moss types.

SPIDELL'S FINE PLANTS
Junction City, OR 97448
African violets and other gesneriads.

STEWART, FRED A., INC.
1212 East Las Tunas Drive, San Gabriel, CA 91778
Orchids and supplies for growing.

SUNNYBROOK FARMS
9448 Mayfield Road, Chesterland, OH 44026
Herbs and house plants.

TINARI GREENHOUSES
2325 Valley Road, Huntington Valley, PA 19006
African violets, related plants, supplies and equipment.

WILSON BROTHERS
Roachdale, IN 46172
Geraniums and other house plants.

YOSHIMURA BONSAI COMPANY, INC.
200 Benedict Avenue, Tarrytown, NY 10591
Bonsai and supplies.

ZIESENHENNE, RUDOLPH
1130 N. Milpas Street, Santa Barbara, CA 93003
Begonias.

Sources for fluorescent lighting equipment

CRAFT-HOUSE MANUFACTURING COMPANY
Wilson, NY 10706
Lighted plant stands.

FLORALITE COMPANY
4124 East Oakwood Road, Oak Creek, WI 53221
Fluorescent fixtures, mist sprayers, tubes, timers, trays, labels, other equipment and growing supplies.

GENERAL ELECTRIC COMPANY
Lamp Division, Nela Park, Cleveland, OH
Manufacturers of fluorescent and incandescent lamps.

HOUSE PLANT CORNER
P.O. Box 810, Oxford, MD 21654
Lighted plant stands, other equipment and all kinds of supplies.

NEAS GROWERS SUPPLY
P.O. Box 8773, Greenville, SC 29604
Table-top light units and other lighting equipment.

SHOPLITE COMPANY
566 Franklin Avenue, Nutley, NJ 07110
All kinds of lighting equipment and supplies.

SYLVANIA ELECTRIC PRODUCTS, INC.
60 Boston Street, Salem, MA 01971
Manufacturers of all types of fluorescent lamps, including growth lamps.

TUBE CRAFT, INC.
1311 West 80th Street, Cleveland, OH 44101
FloraCart and other lighting equipment and supplies.

WESTINGHOUSE ELECTRIC CORPORATION
Westinghouse Lamp Division, Bloomfield, NJ.
Manufacturers of fluorescent lamps.

Sources for home greenhouses

ALUMINUM GREENHOUSES, INC.
14615 Lorain Avenue, Cleveland, OH 44111.

AMERICAN LEISURE INDUSTRIES, INC.
P.O. Box 63, Deep River, CT 06417.

CASA-PLANTA
9489 Dayton Way, Suite 211
Beverly Hills, CA 90210.

GEODESIC DOMES
R.R. 1, Bloomington, IL 61701.

J. A. NEARING COMPANY, INC.
10788 Tucker Street, Beltsville, MD 20705.

LORD & BURNHAM
Irvington, New York, NY 10533.

REDFERN'S PREFAB GREENHOUSES
55 M. Hermon Road, Scotts Valley, CA 95060.

REDWOOD DOMES
2664 Highway 1, Aptos, CA 95003.

PETER REIMULLER
Box 2666, Santa Cruz, CA 95060.

STURDI-BUILT MANUFACTURING COMPANY
11304 S.W. Boones Ferry Road, Portland, OR 97219.

TEXAS GREENHOUSE COMPANY, INC.
2717 St. Louis Avenue, Fort Worth, TX 76110.

TURNER GREENHOUSES
P.O. Box 1260, Goldsboro, NC 27530.

Wooden planter instructions

AMERICAN PLYWOOD ASSOCIATION
1119 A Street, Tacoma, WA 98401.

CALIFORNIA REDWOOD ASSOCIATION
617 Montgomery Street, San Francisco, CA 94111.

Periodicals and Societies devoted to house plants

AFRICAN VIOLET SOCIETY OF AMERICA, INC.
Box 1326, Knoxville, TN 37901
Membership $6.00 yearly includes African Violet Magazine *5 times per year.*

AMERICAN BEGONIA SOCIETY, INC.
1431 Coronado Terrace, Los Angeles, CA 90026
Membership $4.00 per year includes
The Begonia *monthly.*

THE AMERICAN BONSAI SOCIETY
229 North Shore Drive, Lake Waukomis, Parksville, MO 64151
Membership $10.00 per year includes
Bonsai *quarterly.*

AMERICAN FERN SOCIETY
Department of Botany, University of Tennessee
Knoxville, TN 37916
Membership $5.00 per year includes American Fern Journal *quarterly.*

THE AMERICAN FUCHSIA SOCIETY
738-22nd Avenue, San Francisco, CA 94121
Membership $3.00 per year includes American Fuchsia Society Bulletin *monthly.*

THE AMERICAN GLOXINIA AND GESNERIAD SOCIETY, INC.
Department AHS, Eastford, CT 06242
Membership $5.00 per year includes
The Gloxinian *bi-monthly.*

THE AMERICAN PRIMROSE SOCIETY
14015 84th Avenue, NE Bothell, WA 98011
Membership of $5.00 per year includes Quarterly of the American Primrose Society.

CACTUS AND SUCCULENT SOCIETY OF AMERICA, INC.
Box 167, Reseda, CA 91335
Membership $10.00 per year includes Cactus and Succulent Journal *bi-monthly.*

EPIPHYLLUM SOCIETY OF AMERICA
218 E. Graystone Avenue, Monrovia, GA 91016
Membership $2.00 per year includes
Epiphyllum Bulletin *irregular.*

THE AMERICAN ORCHID SOCIETY
Botanical Museum of Harvard University,
Cambridge, MA 02138
Membership $10.00 per year includes American Orchid Society Bulletin *monthly.*

THE AMERICAN PLANT LIFE SOCIETY AND THE AMERICAN AMARYLLIS SOCIETY
Box 150, LaJolla, CA 92037
Membership $5.00 per year includes Plant Life—Amaryllis Yearbook *bulletin.*

THE INDOOR LIGHT GARDENING SOCIETY OF AMERICA, INC.,
4 Wildwood Road, Greenville, SC 29607
Membership $5.00 per year includes Light Garden *bi-monthly.*

THE PALM SOCIETY
7229 SW 54th Avenue, Miami, FL 33143
Membership $10.00 per year includes
Principes *quarterly.*

SAINTPAULIA INTERNATIONAL
Box 10604, Knoxville, TN 37914
Membership $4.00 per year includes Gesneriad Saintpaulia News *bi-monthly.*

PLANTS ALIVE MAGAZINE
2100 N. 45th Street, Seattle, WA 98103
$9.00 yearly.

UNDER GLASS MAGAZINE
Lord and Burnham, Irvington, NY 10533
$2.00 yearly.